MONEY-MAKING
IDEAS
FOR KIDS

TODD TEMPLE and MELINDA DOUROS

OLIVER
NELSON

THOMAS NELSON PUBLISHERS
Nashville · Atlanta · London · Vancouver

To Lou Douros—a born entrepreneur whose enormous
talents belong to God.

Library of Congress Cataloging-in-Publication Data
Temple, Todd, 1958–
    Money-making ideas for kids / Todd Temple and Melinda Douros.
      p.   cm.
    ISBN 0-7852-8260-2 (pbk.)
     1. Children—Finance, Personal. 2. Child rearing. 3. Money-making proj-
ects for children. 4. Entrepreneurship. 5. New business enterprises.
I. Douros, Melinda, 1958–   . II. Title.
HG179.T413 1994
658′.041 dc20   94-190
                                                       CIP

Published in Nashville, Tennessee, by Thomas Nelson, Inc., Publishers, and
distributed in Canada by Word Communications, Ltd., Richmond, British
Columbia.

The Bible version used in this publication is THE NEW KING JAMES
VERSION. Copyright © 1979, 1980, 1982, Thomas Nelson, Inc., Publishers.

Printed in the United States of America.

1 2 3 4 5 6 — 99 98 97 96 95 94

Contents

Introduction

"Hey Mom, can I have some money?"

If you had a dollar for every time your kids have asked this question, you'd be rich. Of course, if they repaid you all the money you gave them in answer, you'd be beyond rich. The question ranks with "What can I do?" as the most popular interrogatives of the typical child's life. This book shows you how to answer both of these persistent questions.

The book contains two sections. The first tells you how to prepare your child for a money-making venture. The chapters cover topics such as safety, money management, and basic business tips.

The second section describes dozens of money-making ventures for kids age eight and older. Of course, you will need to choose ideas that are appropriate to your child's age and talents as well as adapt them to the nature of the neighborhood marketplace where she will conduct her business. Each of these money-making ideas is written directly to the child entrepreneur and gives the following information:

- What You Need: A list of the equipment and supplies necessary to conduct business.
- What to Charge: An estimate of how much the child can charge for the product or service. These are ballpark figures; you will need to help your child set a fee based on expenses, the quality of his service, prices

charged by the competition, and the marketplace's ability to pay for his product or service. Many of the recommended wages exceed minimum wage. Remember that running a business requires time and expense beyond what the child spends on the job site. Record keeping, advertising, customer relations, and other management tasks justify a child entrepreneur's higher wage.

- Find the Customer: What your child will need to do to find and win customers to the business.
- Start Here: A description of the steps involved in starting, running, and growing the business. This section is not a blueprint for conducting the business but rather a summary of the work involved.
- Tricks of the Trade: Quick tips to help your child succeed in the new venture.

Each money-making idea concludes with a section for you, titled "Parental Guidance Suggested." Here we give you suggestions that will help you direct your child to success, not only in the business sense but also in a larger and more important context. An experience like starting a business, at any age, can and will shape enduring values and character. Hence, parents of young entrepreneurs have a unique and enviable opportunity to aid and influence those developments in their children. Your child will need you in the venture. Ultimately, the success of any venture should be measured, not by how much money your child makes but by who he or she becomes as result of the experience.

Note: To simplify the writing, some of the ideas are written to boys, and others are written to girls. Any idea will work for either sex.

PART ONE

===

HELPING
YOUR CHILD
MAKE
MONEY

1

Making Work Safe for Your Child

Look at your child: growing up, starting a business, getting so responsible. Guess your kid doesn't need you so much anymore. Wrong! Now more than ever, your son or daughter needs a parent and not just for applause. Your child needs your protection. His lack of experience in the world puts him at risk to be manipulated, taken advantage of, even seduced. God forbid that it happen, but in today's world the scenario is not impossible. You must embrace fully your role as protector and boldly, unashamedly exercise your prerogatives as his parent. Here are some steps to take.

1. Create an environment in which your son or daughter can speak freely and intimately with you without fear of condemnation or humiliation. Remind him frequently that if any person speaks or behaves towards him in a way that is uncomfortable or intimidating, he needs to tell you immediately. Let him know that you will stand by him in any situation in which he feels threatened. He may act like he doesn't need you, but you both know differently.

2. Openly and appropriately educate your son or daughter about people who, in weakness, prey upon children and young adults whom they perceive as vulnerable. Take advantage of the many resources designed to teach your

child specific skills to avoid or escape threatening situations. No parent likes to intrude upon the innocence of childhood, but it is far better to gently teach your child that some people make terrible choices for terrible reasons than to have her unknowingly fall prey to a sick individual.

3. Never let your child work in the home of someone you have never met. Insist that before he takes on a new customer, you must at least meet and talk with that person. This rule will communicate to your child that you are taking an active role in his protection, and it will communicate to the customer that there is an involved and aware parent attached to this child. Exchange pleasantries, establishing when you will pick up the child and where you can be reached. Don't hesitate to chaperone your child at his workplace if you so choose, and consider dropping in unexpectedly now and then. Even if you are satisfied that your child's customer is safe and healthy, keep all lines of communication open, listening carefully to your child's descriptions of his time on the job. You needn't be always suspicious; just be intensely aware.

4. Supervise your child's record keeping. Make sure she is charging accurately and being paid accurately. By doing so, you will protect her from any accusation of wrongdoing. If a customer questions your child's honesty, you will be fully prepared to help her deal with the situation, having kept yourself informed all along.

5. Call the shots when it comes to issues of safety. Many parents have abdicated their responsibilities to their older children. Never hesitate to put your foot down if you feel that an activity, a location, or a financial transaction puts your child at risk. Your child's business is far more than a tool by which to make money. It is a place to make responsible decisions, to build character, to gain experience, to clarify values. Though he may disagree with your perceptions and your subsequent decisions, don't let that stop

you. You are still his parent, and you must exercise your responsibility as such.

6. Be comfortable with the idea that you have a place in your child's business. Though her venture is certainly a step toward independence, she need not and should not go it alone. Supervising and assisting her will surely take time—time you may not have expected to give. But you will quickly see that the rewards exceed the investment— a good business decision all the way!

2

Is It Wise for Kids to Work?

At age fifteen, Jack London (author of *Call of the Wild*) was working ten-hour days in a cannery for a dollar a day. That was a century ago. Yet even today, in most parts of the world, children work long and hard to support their families and feed themselves. We are fortunate to have a choice in the matter.

The right job experience can have a wonderful effect on a child:

- It shapes the way your child perceives work. A good experience now will make work in the future better. Since he'll probably be working most of his life, it's nice to start off with a healthy perception.
- It can do wonders for your child's self-image. It's a good feeling to know that your customers are depending on you to do a job that you know you can do. The rush of self-confidence may inspire her to accomplish great things in other areas of her life.
- It exposes your child to new people—nice people and not-so-nice people. He'll find himself getting along great with people he'd never have chosen as friends. Suddenly all rules about who's cool and who isn't don't apply.

- Unlike much of what your child learns in school, the things she learns at work are put to use immediately. She won't be learning things to earn a grade, she'll be learning because she knows she needs to learn to succeed.

A job can be a positive experience. But it can also leave its mark in negative ways:

- Too much work during the school year will hurt your child's education.
- Your child may lose valuable time for friends, sports, church, music, or other important parts of his life.
- Your child will earn money, and money can stir up an appetite to acquire more and more material things.

LABOR LAWS

Many jobs can be hazardous to your child's physical health. Childhood is an inherently dangerous occupation; a child performing a dangerous task is doubly hazardous. It's also illegal. Because of the abuses suffered by Jack London and countless other children in history, our society has passed laws that limit the kinds of jobs kids can perform and how many hours they can work.

The Fair Labor Standards Act is a federal law affecting anyone under eighteen. It says that children can't work during school hours or perform dangerous work—operate dangerous machinery, work up on scaffolding, or be exposed to "adult" vices.

For children under sixteen, the above restrictions apply as well as a few more: they can't work more than three hours on a school day, work past seven o'clock at night, or put in more than eighteen hours during a week.

Each state has its own labor laws, which may be stricter than the federal law. Although the federal law doesn't require a child to have a work permit, your state may. (You can get the facts by calling the Employment or Labor office listed under the State Government section of your phone book.)

YOUR CALL

As with everything else in your child's life, you have the privilege and duty to decide if working is right for your son or daughter. Sit down together and talk about the effect a job will have on her life. The discussion will help to ensure that you make the right decision. What's more, it will show her the importance of careful consideration in making choices—knowledge that will have an even greater impact on her life than the decision itself.

3
Shaping Your Child's Money Values

A father brought his ten-year-old son to a trade show where the father's company had an exhibit. The dad couldn't leave the exhibit area for hours on end, so when he got thirsty, he asked his son to run upstairs and get a soda from a vending machine. The enterprising young man realized that there was money to be made in this situation. He went from booth to booth, asking trapped exhibitors if they wanted something to drink. For a dollar, he explained, he would run upstairs, get the drink (which cost seventy-five cents), and deliver it to the thirsty customer.

By the second day, the boy had collected about fifteen dollars and had earned the admiration of the exhibitors, who were impressed by his business intelligence and initiative. But on the last day of the show, this crafty entrepreneur lost both. He spent his entire stack of quarters on cheap plastic charms and toys dispensed from another vending machine. What a waste. The remarkable thing was that the father didn't stop him. He could have held onto his son's money until the buying impulse subsided. He could have made his son deposit the money into a savings account. He could have lectured his son on the worthlessness of his purchases. Instead, he let his son throw away his money. Smart dad.

The dad let his son experience the reality of work and its rewards. If the boy was pleased with his decisions, then he fully enjoyed the fruit of his labor. If he was ultimately disappointed in the reward, then he will likely make a better decision the next time he works so hard.

Who knows? Someday, if the lesson learned prevents him from throwing away thousands of dollars on a flashy but unreliable car, then the fifteen dollars in trinkets will have been a wise investment.

If you have not yet had a similar experience with your child, you will—especially if he begins to earn money through one of the ideas in this book. As a parent, it's tough to sit back and watch children make unwise buying decisions. The scene brings back memories of our own poor decisions, and our instincts compel us to prevent our children from making the same mistakes. But some lessons don't stick until our kids experience them personally. Decisions about money and value fit in this category. Teach your child consciously and diligently a godly perspective on money; then allow him the freedom to learn while it's still relatively safe to do so.

MODELING WISE MONEY HABITS

You've been shaping your child's money values from the time you first wheeled your baby through the supermarket. If you're an impulsive buyer, you've been modeling that habit to your child. If you are a careful spender who reads labels, compares prices, and shops around, your child has seen that too. Now that she has money to spend, you'll see the results of your modeling in living color.

Consider bringing your child into the decision-making process on some future purchases. If you're thinking about buying a bicycle, car, camera, or washing machine, talk to her about the issues involved:

- Discuss why you chose one model over another; how you discovered the differences; how you made up your mind.
- Ask your child's opinion: If the decision were his to make, which model would he buy? Why?
- When a purchase will significantly rearrange the family budget, tell your child how.
- Ask: Is the purchase worth the change in the family's life-style?
- How will the purchase affect your life? Is it worth it? Are there alternatives?

In other words, take your child behind the scenes to observe all that takes place before the wallet or the checkbook comes out.

LESSONS WITH YOUR CHILD'S MONEY

As your child begins to earn and spend her own money, you can shape her decision-making abilities simply through conversation. When she gets paid for a job, ask her how she feels about the work and about the reward. Here are questions that can help her weigh the value of her work:

- What did you enjoy about the work?
- What was the least enjoyable part of the job?
- How did you feel when you got paid?
- Do you feel that the work was worth what you got paid?
- Do you think the customer felt the money was worth the work you performed?
- What are some of the things you could do with the money?
- What do you think God wants you to do with your money?
- What will you do with the money? Why is this choice a good deal for you?

- What would you like to do with the money you earn in the future?

When your child makes a purchase with his own money, withhold your judgment on his purchase and talk about his decision:

- How do you feel now that the money is spent?
- Was the reward worth the work? Why?
- If you had the decision to make again, would you do the same thing?
- If you were to earn that much money again, how would you spend it?

CHEAP LESSONS

Chances are your child will make plenty of unwise money decisions as he grows up—and, most likely, not a few as an adult. But there will never be a less expensive time to make those mistakes. The cost of these bad investments is low in terms of dollars and the return is high in terms of opportunity to learn from them. Now is the time to let your child learn the value of earned money.

4

Money Management Made Simple

The overwhelming number of books and magazine articles devoted to money management can give you the impression that the subject is too complicated to understand and certainly too difficult to explain to your children. Actually, the basics of wise money management are simple.

Here are four money principles that anyone can understand. Take a few minutes to read these principles; then share them with your child. As he begins to earn money, he can put them into practice.

By the way, the principles will make more sense if he sees you abiding by them too. Take a moment after reading this chapter to consider what you as an adult might do to manage your money in these ways.

Principle #1: Invest in Things That Go Up in Value

Every dollar you spend is an investment: what you buy with it either goes up or down in value. The moment you buy a car, bicycle, a pair of shoes, or a pair of sunglasses, you start losing money because you can't resell those items for what you paid. You not only start losing that money when you buy the item; you also lose the money you would have gained by investing in something that goes up in value. This loss of income is called *opportunity cost*.

If you want to save money, avoid spending it on things that go down in value. Put as much of it as you can into investments that go up in value. One of the best ways to invest is to spend it on things that will help you make more money. The investment your child makes in tools to conduct a business fits into this category.

Principle #2: Never Borrow Money to Pay for Things That Go Down in Value

Now we're hitting close to home. When you borrow money to purchase something that's losing value, you lose money in three ways. First, the item will never be worth what you paid for it. Second, you incur opportunity cost— what you would be making had you invested in a savings account, for example. And third, you're paying someone to let you borrow the money, i.e., interest.

If you're trying to save money, don't borrow it to buy a depreciating item. While the bank is paying you 2 or 3 percent interest on the money you lend them (with your savings account), you're paying the bank or some other lender 6 to 10 percent interest for the right to borrow it back. Does this sound ridiculous to you? It should! It's like trying to go up the down escalator.

Most people don't follow this advice. They buy on credit and lose in interest charges some or all of the gain in their appreciating investments. Do your kids a favor and break with tradition. Pay cash for things that depreciate, even if it means driving a car without that new-car smell. Show your child that the reward for work well done comes after the work is done, not before.

Principle #3: Invest in Things That Outperform Inflation

Even if you invest in something that goes up in value, inflation can still make you lose money. Inflation is the tendency of prices to rise, making a dollar worth less as time goes on. A 5 percent annual inflation rate might cause a loaf of bread that cost $1.00 last year to run you $1.05; same number of slices, same silly face on the wrapper, just five cents higher in price. So if you have $100.00 invested for a year in a money-market account that yields 5 percent, you now have $105.00. Last year your $100.00 could have bought 100 loaves of bread. This year your $105.00 will buy you the same thing: 100 loaves of bread. You didn't lose money, but you also didn't gain any: you have the same purchasing power you started with.

The worst investment your child can make is putting money in a piggy bank. The value of the money your child has hidden in the sock beneath his third dresser drawer will shrink by the rate of inflation. If your child has begun to make money regularly, teach him how inflation works and help him open a bank account that will beat it.

Principle #4: Make an Appreciating Investment Every Month

Lots of people plan to start investing as soon as they have "enough." But unless you win the lottery or rob a bank, you probably won't suddenly have one big chunk to invest. Instead, you have to invest small amounts for several months and years before it becomes a big investment.

This step-by-step growth principle applies to just about everything in life: use money as a model to teach your child how it works.

THE TIME IS NOW

It's tempting to look at the small sums your child might be earning from her business endeavors and think that it would be easier to teach these principles in a few years, when her income is greater and she can see significant effects on her money. Yet this is precisely why you should start teaching these things now. The effects of interest, inflation, and regular investing are cumulative: build the habits now, then show the clear result of these habits as she grows. And if you start to live by these principles yourself, she'll have a model for wise money management when it's time for her to fend for herself.

5

Banking for Kids

Your child probably already has a savings account. But if she starts up a business, you may want to open a checking account for her. A checking account is especially helpful if her business requires the frequent purchase of supplies and a regular flow of income.

A separate account for business also allows the savings account to remain "sacred"—reinforcing the idea that filling out a withdrawal slip should be a rare and carefully considered act. She'll thank you for instilling that belief when it comes time to buy a car or pay for college.

MINOR PROBLEMS

Opening a checking account for your child can be tricky business. According to the government, contractual agreements made with minors can't be enforced against the minor. These laws are designed to protect children from being hurt by bad deals. The downside is that many banks and other concerns won't do business with minors because they get left holding the bag if the minor fails to deliver.

For example, if you overdraw your checking account by five hundred dollars and refuse to pay back the money, the bank can take you to court to make you pay. If your child were to do the same thing, the court wouldn't recognize the agreement between him and the bank as a legal contract—and the bank would lose its money.

This doesn't mean banks can't do business with a minor —they just don't have the law to protect them if the kid goes astray. Consequently, most banks won't go out of their way to serve minors. On rare occasions, if you're a very good customer of the bank (i.e., if you deposit loads of money there), they may be willing to let your child open a checking account. More likely, they'll require that you be a signer on the account. That means if your progeny skips off to Paris on a bad check, you'll be making good on the funds.

By the way, credit unions tend to be more appreciative of younger customers. If your bank's policy is too restrictive, you may want to pursue this option.

BIG INTEREST

If your child begins to accumulate money, you may want to encourage her to open an interest-bearing account that pays a higher rate than a basic passbook savings account. A certificate of deposit (CD) or money-market account will help her get more for her money. Unfortunately, the minimum deposit on these accounts is often one thousand dollars—a pretty high figure for most kids (and for some of us adults).

Here are two tricks you can use to help your child qualify for one of these premium accounts:

- *Pooling:* Have your child find one or two friends with some money to invest. Put in identical amounts and set up the account so that they all have to sign for any withdrawals. At the end of the deposit period, divide the principal and interest evenly. (This plan is just a small-scale version of a mutual fund.)
- *Bumping:* Bumping is similar to pooling, except that

your child is just using someone else's money to bump her into the "big leagues." You (or another relative) with money in the bank can let her use a few hundred dollars for a bump if she agrees to pay you the portion of the interest your money earns. For example, if you put in $700.00 to bump her $300.00, have her pay you 70 percent of the yield. Ask her to keep track of the money and to repay it when her savings can stand on its own.

GOOD START

Whatever accounts your child opens, show her how to manage them. Children are remarkably quick studies at banking and can often balance a checkbook better than an adult. Maybe this happens because they're working with arithmetic daily at school. Or maybe it's because they don't contend with the negative numbers that come with overdrawn adulthood.

6

Teach Your Child What the Bible Says About Work

Much of the reason we want to see kids work is so that they will

- grow in character
- learn to take responsibility
- develop lifelong skills
- embrace self-discipline
- strive for excellence
- make a difference in the world
- fill their lives with purpose and meaning.

We're in good company. The Bible makes it clear that God feels the same way about the reasons *we* work. Teach your child what the Bible says about doing work and doing it well. Proclaim, upon the Word of God, that while money-making has its place, a person of character and integrity is of far more value to the world and to God's purposes than a person of wealth.

As your child goes about beginning a new business venture, lead him in a study of God's principles of work and His love of excellence. Here are some Scripture verses to get you started.

Principle #1: Work Is God's Gift to Us

So God created man in His own image; in the image of God He created him; male and female He created them. Then God blessed them, and God said to them, "Be fruitful and multiply; fill the earth and subdue it; have dominion over the fish of the sea, over the birds of the air, and over every living thing that moves on the earth."—Genesis 1:27–28

Discuss also John 5:17.

Principle #2: Work Meets Our Needs

For you yourselves know how you ought to follow us, for we were not disorderly among you; nor did we eat anyone's bread free of charge, but worked with labor and toil night and day, that we might not be a burden to any of you . . . For even when we were with you, we commanded you this: If anyone will not work, neither shall he eat.—2 Thessalonians 3:7–8, 10

Principle #3: Work Develops Character

He who is faithful in what is least is faithful also in much; and he who is unjust in what is least is unjust also in much. Therefore if you have not been faithful in the unrighteous mammon, who will commit to your trust the true riches?—Luke 16:10–11

Discuss also Proverbs 10:9.

Who is a person of character?

- Someone who keeps promises—Psalm 15:4
- Someone who meets deadlines—Proverbs 18:9
- Someone who can work without supervision—Ephesians 6:6–7
- Someone who can control money—Luke 16:11

Principle #4: Work Allows Generosity

Let him who stole steal no longer, but rather let him labor, working with his hands what is good, that he may have something to give him who has need.—Ephesians 4:28

Discuss also 1 Thessalonians 4:11–12 and Proverbs 3:9–10. Talk about *tithing*. Discuss what it is and how it works in your family.

Principle #5: Work Is an Example to Others

Aspire to lead a quiet life, to mind your own business, and to work with your own hands, as we commanded you, that you may walk properly toward those who are outside, and that you may lack nothing.—1 Thessalonians 4:11–12

Discuss also Matthew 5:13–16, Romans 12:16–18, Ephesians 4:28, and 1 Corinthians 16:14. Discuss, in light of these verses, how to exemplify cooperation, fairness, flexibility, humility, teamwork, and compromise.

Principle #6: Work Brings Self-Respect

Do you see a man who excels in his work? He will stand before kings.—Proverbs 22:29

Discuss also Proverbs 12:24, Proverbs 16:3, and Colossians 3:24.

Principle #7: Work Develops Perseverance

We also glory in tribulations, knowing that tribulation produces perseverance; and perseverance, character; and character, hope.—Romans 5:3–4

Discuss also Proverbs 20:30, 2 Corinthians 1:8–9, Philippians 2:14–15, Matthew 25:21, Proverbs 22:13, and Proverbs 13:4.

Principle #8: Work Allows Us to Serve Others

For we are His workmanship, created in Christ Jesus for good works, which God prepared beforehand that we should walk in them.—Ephesians 2:10

Discuss also Titus 3:14, Mark 8:35, Philippians 2:4–5, Matthew 20:28, Proverbs 3:27–28, 1 Corinthians 15:58, and Matthew 20:26.

IT IS GOOD TO EXCEL IN YOUR WORK

People who excel work with enthusiasm. See Ephesians 6:7–8, Colossians 3:2–3, Ecclesiastes 9:9–10, Proverbs 22:29, and Proverbs 26:16.

People who excel develop their skills. See Proverbs 16:20; 15:14; 18:15; and Ecclesiastes 10:10.

People who excel keep their word. See Proverbs 20:6; 25:19; 12:3; 10:9; and Colossians 3:22.

People who excel cooperate with others. See Ecclesiastes 4:9–12 and Proverbs 27:17.

People who excel do more than is expected. See Matthew 5:41–42, Proverbs 22:13, and Proverbs 13:4. Read the story of Eleazar and Rebekah in Genesis 24. Talk about what happened to Rebekah when she did what she was asked and then did a little bit more.

Special thanks to pastor Ron Thompson, Twin Cities Community Church, Nevada City, California, for some of the ideas used in this chapter.

PART TWO

MONEY-MAKING
IDEAS
FOR
KIDS

7

Make Buttons

WHAT YOU NEED

- advertising fliers
- button-making machine (compact, approximately $30.00, available through specialty advertising catalogs; your local party supply store will know where to find them)
- designs (created by you or provided by your client)
- access to a copy machine (for making multiple designs)
- Polaroid camera (optional, for making photo-buttons on-site at carnivals, sports tournaments, and other special events)

WHAT TO CHARGE

Figure out what your supplies cost for each button. If your client has provided the design, charge $.50 per button, above and beyond your costs. If you have created the design, charge $1.00 per button beyond your costs. For photo-buttons, charge $3.00.

FIND THE CUSTOMER

Announce your new venture with creative fliers, distributing them to potential customers:

- at school clubs
- at libraries
- to political groups
- to nonprofit agencies
- to church youth groups

- at restaurants
- at theaters
- at small and large businesses

All of these organizations can use buttons. Consider buying booth space at a carnival or other community event. Take Polaroid photos on-site and make photo-buttons. Join forces with a face painter and offer a double deal. Go to sports events and make team buttons. Offer your services to restaurants or party stores for personalized "Happy Birthday" buttons.

START HERE

Make an appointment with your potential client, showing him your price list, turn-around time (each button takes about a minute to assemble), and some sample buttons. If you get an order, write it on a preprinted order form, keeping it on a clipboard or in a special file. You may want to request half your fee at the time of order and the other half upon delivery.

If you don't get an order, ask when you might call again and if your customer might give you a referral. Be sure to thank him for his time. You might ask if he has children, and if so, give him a button that says "Kids are Great!"

Make sure you always deliver on time and that you treat every client with respect. Your good reputation will follow you, and you will be surprised at your success.

TRICKS OF THE TRADE

Buttons are meant to be noticed. Here's how to draw attention to your business and products:

- Use bright colors and big, bold type.
- Cover yourself with buttons and wear them to a community event.
- Create buttonwear—button hats, button shoes, button necklaces!
- Make a giant button sign from the clear head of a bass drum.
- Select your own Teacher of the Month by awarding a teacher with a button that says so.

PARENTAL GUIDANCE SUGGESTED

Encourage your child to develop relationships with her customers. Stop in with her to say hello to her clients when you're near their place of business. Help her write thank-you notes when someone makes a referral. Developing these relationships and learning to communicate with professional adults will be a boon to her self-confidence and identity, and these skills may facilitate significant opportunities for future employment.

Help her enjoy her work. When she is making buttons, play her favorite music or work next to her and enjoy some conversation. After she finishes, celebrate. Go to the pool, get ice cream, or watch a movie together. Teach her that rest after effort is good rest.

8

Clean Cages

Housecleaner needed. Appealing clients, though charming and colorful, can be messy. Job requires gentleness, loving care. Must enjoy birds, gerbils, rabbits, kitties, fish, and certain humans.

WHAT YOU NEED

- advertising fliers
- telephone
- pair of gloves
- pet treats
- a trash bag and rags (the customer can provide sawdust or kitty litter as needed)

WHAT TO CHARGE

$5.00 per cage per cleaning.

FIND THE CUSTOMER

Take your fliers to pet stores, veterinarian offices, retirement homes, and schools. Go door to door, offering a free trial cleaning and leaving a pet treat (carrots for rabbits and guinea pigs, seed sticks for birds, a bag of worms for fish).

START HERE

To learn the most efficient, safe, and thorough way to clean a small animal cage, ask your local pet store owner or vet for a lesson. After having been well instructed, you might ask to leave fliers that explain your special service in the store or office. Perhaps your instructor might recommend you to her own customers.

When talking with a potential customer, bring along an appointment book and some business cards. If the customer decides to give your service a try, immediately write the appointment in your book and write it on a card for your client. You want her to know you are serious about keeping your appointments!

When cleaning the cage, be especially careful not to make a mess on the floor. Be prepared to thoroughly clean up any spills. You may want to have the pet owner remove the animal from the cage to avoid harming either yourself or the pet. You don't want to spend your afternoon chasing a chinchilla through the house. Don't forget to bring a treat to keep your animal friends happy.

TRICKS OF THE TRADE

Here are the qualities and manners of a truly great cage cleaner:

- Call your customers' animals by their names.
- Never complain out loud about the smell.
- Treat every pet as if it were your own.
- Pick up every last bit of sawdust, kitty litter, or shredded paper.

- If a customer's pet should escape during a cage cleaning, catch it quick!

PARENTAL GUIDANCE SUGGESTED

Your child is learning to care for both pets and people. Encourage him to recognize what pleasure his service brings to both and applaud him for his gentle kindness. Consider accompanying your child on any visits to new clients, both to evaluate the environment in which he may be working and to provide added support as your child completes his task.

Remember: think beyond dirty cages. Your child is learning responsibility, accountability, and communication skills. Guide him with patience and enthusiasm by helping him see his work from your broader perspective.

Point out the specific skills you see him acquiring. Verbalize every detail of his success. Let him know that his efforts are something he can take pride in. By concentrating on the positive, you will motivate him to continue to step out into responsible independence, giving him one of the greatest gifts a parent can give.

9

Make Balloon Bouquets

Cheerful young entrepreneur needed to liven up various celebrations by providing balloon bouquets. Must enjoy creative decoration.

WHAT YOU NEED

- advertising fliers or business cards
- a telephone for customers to call
- helium tank (purchased for approximately $20.00 at a party supply store or warehouse store)
- a variety of balloons (purchased at a party supply store or bought in bulk from a wholesaler)
- colorful ribbon

WHAT TO CHARGE

$.50 for helium balloons, $.25 for air-filled. For any specialty styles, double the cost of materials.

FIND THE CUSTOMER

Try giveaways! Everyone loves to get a balloon. Give away lots of yours, each with a business card or small flier attached to the string. Perhaps you could write your business name and phone number on some of your balloons with a felt-tip pen.

Distribute balloons at fairs, parades, even (with permission) in front of the grocery store. Make appointments with event coordinators, offering your services to people in charge of birthday parties, weddings, banquets, conferences, meetings, open houses, sales events, school occasions, or any other gathering you can think of. Go door to door in your neighborhood, tying your floating ad to each doorknob with a flier attached.

If you read about an upcoming event in the newspaper, call the person in charge and tell him about your business. If your balloons are used to enhance a theme party (black and white balloons at a formal affair; pink and blue at a baby shower; red, white, and blue at a Fourth of July picnic), take a picture and build a portfolio to show your potential customers. Learn to make balloon arches and sell them regularly to car dealerships.

Your potential customers in this business are limitless. Be bold, organized, and polite and your business will grow and grow!

TRICKS OF THE TRADE

When it comes to balloon bouquets, you're the expert! Here's what professionals do when their customers come by for business:

- Express enthusiasm for the celebration you're helping to decorate.
- Offer suggestions about colors and styles.

- Give a balloon to any small children accompanying your customer.
- Help the customer wrangle a bouquet of balloons into her car and cheerfully replace any that pop in the process.

PARENTAL GUIDANCE SUGGESTED

This business affords your child the opportunity to meet and deal with many, many clients. He will need to become skilled in phone manners, in listening skills, and in organization. Help him keep careful records of his orders and deadlines and take pride in watching his confidence grow as he manages his endeavor successfully. Avoid becoming a full-time delivery service; let your child arrange for the client to pick up the balloon order at your home. For very large orders, you may want to transport your child and his supplies to the event site. Remember, for maximum flotation, balloons must be delivered within twenty-four hours.

10
Distribute Fliers

Kinetic young person needed to deliver
advertising fliers door to door for small
businesses. Must love to walk or ride a
bike.

WHAT YOU NEED

- [ ] your own advertising fliers
- [ ] a backpack or bag to carry your deliveries
- [ ] sturdy shoes

WHAT TO CHARGE

$10.00 per 100 fliers; more for a rural area.

FIND THE CUSTOMER

Circulate your fliers among small businesses, particularly targeting nonprofit organizations: crisis pregnancy centers, health care clinics, political organizations, religious organizations, arts programs, and counseling centers. These types of organizations often cannot afford to send out mass mailings to the community where, in fact, their services and information may be desperately needed. By charging considerably less to hand deliver than it may cost to mail advertising material, you are doing these organizations and others a favor and creating a business for yourself.

You might encourage local merchants to try some creative advertising using your delivery service. You could pass out suckers from the local candy store or sugarless gum from the dentist. You could deliver one free sandwich a day to someone in an office complex near the sandwich shop. You could even distribute menus one day, take orders and deliver lunch the next.

START HERE

Agree with your customer on the method of delivery; you could hang fliers on the doorknob, place them under the welcome mat, toss them in the driveway, etc. Offer, for triple the charge, to knock on the door of each house and deliver a sales pitch for the product or service advertised.

Every time you make deliveries, wear a bright T-shirt with the name of your delivery service boldly printed on the front and back. As your neighbors become familiar with your efficient service, good manners, cheerful disposition, and maybe even the goodies you bring, they too will be likely to call upon you for service.

TRICKS OF THE TRADE

Success in business is never easy. Yet it's easy to add simple gestures to your hard work to help make success happen:

- Wave or say hello to everyone you see in the neighborhood.
- Learn the names of as many neighbors as you can—then

address them by their names: say, "Hello, Mrs. Martinez," or "Good afternoon, Mr. Kleppman."

- Remember small courtesies, like picking up the newspaper and carrying it to the front door, closing a gate behind you, or not stepping on the plants.

PARENTAL GUIDANCE SUGGESTED

Your child will learn and grow from his interaction with many different business owners and managers. You can greatly enhance his popularity simply by teaching him social graces. Polite children are increasingly rare, so they carry a mark of distinction. Your child, having gracious speech and deference to his elders, will win many friends in the community and will himself deserve respect. Let him know that success in business is more closely tied to social skills than most people will admit and that honoring those he works for is effective and right.

Though unlikely, you may run into a situation where your child is asked to distribute material with which you are uncomfortable. If this indeed happens, accept it as golden opportunity to discuss and decide with your child what he should do. Don't allow him to handle immoral or tasteless material, but do help him to communicate his standards respectfully to his client, an experience he will likely draw upon in years to come.

11

Wash Sheets and Towels

Dependable person needed to strip beds, wash dirty sheets and towels, and replace them when clean. No experience necessary. Must be good listener, prompt, and friendly.

WHAT YOU NEED

Not much—just your advertising fliers and your willingness to help people who may not have the time or physical ability to do this job.

WHAT TO CHARGE

For service once a week, charge $20.00 per month. Plan on spending about two hours per house.

FIND THE CUSTOMER

Creative advertising will help you build your customer base. Consider designing a flier targeted to young families that says something like this: "Who would you rather cuddle up to—your kids or your washing machine? Spend an extra two hours a week enjoying your children while your dirty sheets and towels are laundered and replaced by an honest, hardworking kid."

Distribute a different message to your elderly neighbors or even to people with back problems for whom changing a bed is a serious challenge. Say something like "Retire from a backbreaking chore. Let a hardworking and enthusiastic kid launder and replace your sheets and towels, saving you time and energy for more relaxing things."

Take your fliers door to door, offering a free trial to the wary.

Perhaps you can ask apartment complex managers, especially those who have many elderly tenants, to display your flier in the office. You may even contact chiropractors or orthopedists whose clients may be temporarily or permanently disabled and in need of your help.

START HERE

Each customer will have a unique way of doing laundry. At your first appointment have your customer teach you to use her machines properly and to wash, fold, and rearrange the bed linens to her specifications. You would be wise to note the details in a small notebook so that you will remember them the following week.

Either bring something to read while waiting through the wash and dry cycles or organize your schedule so that you can service more than one house at a time. Work quietly and efficiently and always be prompt. Your customers will be grateful for the service you provide and impressed with your maturity.

Chances are your customers will refer you to friends. If so, bring a small gift of thanks (like potpourri, nice soaps, or a small fruit basket).

TRICKS OF THE TRADE

Your service relieves customers from a long, tedious job. Here are some ways you can make the job more enjoyable for yourself and your customers:

- Learn the fastest and best way to fold. Fitted sheets provide a special challenge. Ask a professional launderer to show you how to fold them neatly and efficiently.
- If the customer has small children, ask if you can bring them inexpensive treats—stickers, a pencil, a little bag of bite-size crackers.
- Always be on your best behavior—especially while you wait for the washer and dryer to do their work.

PARENTAL GUIDANCE SUGGESTED

We know what you're thinking: "I can't even get him to make his own bed, much less strip and wash and fold and . . ." Remember, somehow doing someone else's chores feels different to a kid—or to anyone, for that matter.

Regardless of the frustration you may feel about family jobs, encourage your child to develop a business. Help him feel capable; applaud his efforts. Build on the sense of mastery he will gain as he completes these tasks outside the home. The foundation built by your support will undoubtedly bear fruit as your increasingly self-directed child learns to accept responsibility. Who knows? Someday, he may even pick up his socks.

12

Make Wake-Up Calls

Utterly dependable, consistently genial early-riser needed to phone customers each morning with a greeting, a weather report, and a summary of the top news stories of the day.

WHAT YOU NEED

- advertising fliers
- telephone
- newspaper subscription
- two alarm clocks (for yourself!)

WHAT TO CHARGE

$10.00 per month, prepaid.

FIND THE CUSTOMER

Target both your neighborhood and the business community with your fliers, always emphasizing that it is far better to awaken to a friendly voice communicating helpful information than it is to awaken to an intrusive, annoying, obnoxious, wholly unpleasant beep or buzz.

START HERE

Agree with your customer on the time of your call and on the days a wake-up call is desired. Let him know that you will greet him, report the weather forecast, and give a short overview of the morning's top news in less than a minute. Consider offering to read your customers a Bible verse in addition to or instead of the morning's news.

Each morning get up a half hour before your first call. Write out the morning's information on an index card so that you are able to communicate it quickly and concisely to your customers. Your business will succeed if you are unfailingly dependable.

TRICKS OF THE TRADE

- Use a warm and friendly voice. Don't let embarrassment turn you into a monotone.
- Carefully consider what you say. Ask for help at first, identifying the right news stories to report, the right Bible verses to share.
- Occasionally, send a handwritten note to thank the customer for giving your business a chance.

PARENTAL GUIDANCE SUGGESTED

This job is a sure exercise in responsibility. Tempting as it may be to wake up the wake-up caller, try to let your child shoulder the full weight of his commitment. You can make sure he knows that laxity on his part may have serious consequences for his customers, but otherwise talk positively about the helpful and pleasant service he is providing for his community.

13

Grow Vegetables and Herbs

Lover of the outdoors needed to grow fresh, healthy vegetables or herbs to sell directly to neighbors and friends. May expand into fruits, canned and fresh, and other homegrown goodies.

WHAT YOU NEED

- plot of ground to cultivate—or containers for smaller-scale gardening
- tools and gardening supplies appropriate to the size and content of your garden
- wheelbarrow or wagon with which to peddle your produce

WHAT TO CHARGE

Just a tad less than the grocery store happens to be charging.

FIND THE CUSTOMER

It's hard to imagine anyone turning down the offer of fresh, homegrown vegetables or herbs, especially from a kid on the doorstep pulling a wagonful. Let your potential customer know about the attributes of your produce. It's fresher, it was grown organically, it's cheaper, and it's on your doorstep. Who could turn it down?

START HERE

Chances are, if this idea interests you, you already know something about gardening. Don't hesitate to ask for help from any experts around you. (Check out Mom and Dad first.)

Successful gardeners are full of crucial information. Growing fruits and veggies can take a lot of time initially, but the investment will really pay off, barring any early freezes or floods. Consider starting small and growing slowly but steadily—just like your plants. You might concentrate at first on growing just fresh herbs. You might circulate a flier just before your harvest so that your neighbors will be ready to buy when you're ready to sell. Gardening is a wonderful and satisfying pastime and can make you some considerable money to boot.

TRICKS OF THE TRADE

- Make sure your produce looks good. Rinse it off and arrange it nicely. Remember, shoppers are used to waxed apples and misty lettuce. You need to impress their eyes before you can impress their mouths.
- Be ready to describe your gardening method. Know what substances have been in contact with your produce. Customers may want to know about fertilizers, herbicides, insecticides, etc.
- Call your county health department to make sure you do not need a permit to sell your produce. In most places you won't. What you do need is a thorough un-

derstanding of proper food handling. When selling produce you must be conscientious about keeping your hands clean to prevent the spread of disease. Ask your health department representative what else you should know to ensure your customers' health and safety.

PARENTAL GUIDANCE SUGGESTED

Gardeners seem to breed gardeners. If you possess the skill and knowledge necessary to the growing of superior produce, give your child the great gift of your experience. Work together with her, planning and problem-solving. Soon enough she will be on her own and will truly reap what she sows—a lifelong lesson that we all must learn.

You will be helping her to develop a skill that is not only marketable but potentially life-saving as well. In a time when so many have lost touch with the earth and have no inkling of the joy inherent in growing things, you have a particular opportunity to contribute to the world at large by the simple help you give your budding gardener.

If you are not the gardening type, dive in with your child. Check out library books, query friends, experiment together. What healthier way could you spend time with your offspring? Set aside your chores a while and enjoy the opportunity to be a partner in learning with one of the most beloved people in your life.

14

Make Stationery

WHAT YOU NEED

There are many ways to make stationery. Use leaf
prints, pressed flowers, calligraphy, drawings, stencils,
rubber stamps; find books in the library that will help you
and pick the style you like. Before you make your final
choice, think about how much you can spend on materials
and how much time each type of design will take. Have
fun experimenting!

WHAT TO CHARGE

Package your stationery and envelopes in sets of 20.
Charge $3.75 per pack, making adjustments for styles re-
quiring costlier materials. Or set your price by adding all
your costs and doubling them.

FIND THE CUSTOMER

Make ten to twenty sets of stationery to test the market. Go to local stationery stores, drugstores, souvenir shops —anyplace you have access to—that could sell your product. You can sell direct or on consignment.

If you sell direct, the store owner buys the stationery from you and sells it again at a higher price. If you sell on consignment, you give the stationery to the store owner and wait for the store's customers to buy it. If they do, you collect your money, giving some back to the store owner for letting you use her store space. Both methods will make you about the same amount of money.

Selling on consignment is safer for the store since the owner isn't stuck with the merchandise if it doesn't sell. Selling direct is safer for you because once you sell to the store you don't have to worry about individual customers buying the product. You and the store owner will have to negotiate this issue.

START HERE

Your stationery is likely to sell better if it's personalized —the name of your town, a picture of a historical place, a special statement. You might also package it in a way that lets the buyer know it was made by a kid. For example, if you do calligraphy, write Bible verses on multi-colored paper with a paper band around the package that says, "KidCallig—designs by Ashley, age 11."

Or you could use rubber stamp designs of animals. Color the stamp designs with markers and have them shrink-wrapped. Add a sticker on the front that says, for example, "Kids for the Earth—designs by Michael and Matthew, ages 8 and 12."

Be prepared to fill orders on time and keep track of what you sell. If your stationery business really takes off, you may want to hire an assistant to help with production and distribution. A graphic artist or printer would probably have some good information to share with you—where to buy cheap or bulk supplies, how to keep costs down, reproduction and packaging ideas, and even selling tips.

You can manufacture and sell any craft item—bookmarks, earrings, hair bows, Christmas ornaments, baby bibs—the sky's the limit!

TRICKS OF THE TRADE

- Present your product with confidence. Let that store owner know that your handiwork is a worthwhile addition to her inventory. Don't be shy!
- Print extra sets of popular stationery so you can fill orders quickly.
- Continue to expand and explore new projects and techniques.

PARENTAL GUIDANCE SUGGESTED

Patient encouragement of your child's artistic bent, no matter how humble, is a profound act of love. Many children grow up never discovering the treasure store of talent inside. On the other hand, nurturing an artistic child's business savvy is an equally valuable effort.

Many right-brained thinkers have a difficult time with the linear thinking and organizational skills associated with business practice. As a result, artists can flounder for a lifetime, unable to advance themselves in the public sphere. A balanced development of abstract, conceptual ability with an understanding of and discipline for business will give your child untold advantages in the world.

This enterprise is a starting place for exactly that development.

Help your child hone her skill in whatever craft she chooses. Help her to keep clean, consistent records. Help her to think through her business practices, using your collective math skills to determine whether or not she is truly turning a profit and how she can improve her earnings. Take her to craft fairs and help her strike up conversations with exhibitors. Save pertinent articles; offer to pay for a class in art or business at a community education center.

Help her as well to deal politely and humbly with her customers. The whole experience will be invaluable and serve her well for years to come.

15
Maintain Computer Files

WHAT YOU NEED

☐ business cards or fliers

WHAT TO CHARGE

$5.00 per visit. If your visit lasts more than half an hour because you're servicing multiple computers, charge more.

FIND THE CUSTOMER

Because you are advertising solely to the business community and proposing to deal with pivotal computer systems, it is important to posture yourself as an incredibly responsible kid. Consider having business cards printed or even a resumé detailing your activities and accomplishments. Stress those areas in which you have shown responsibility (Scout leadership, student government, academic achievement, etc.).

List specifically your computer experience and write a short paragraph explaining why you can be trusted with this job. Include a quote from a teacher or community leader in your support. Go door to door in the business community, asking first to meet with the office manager. Explain your service, promising to label and store the disks or tapes you copy. Emphasize the advantages of having safe and organized storage of material by a responsible person focused solely on that single task.

START HERE

Many people back up hard disk files on a weekly basis, some back up every day. Find out how often your customer wants your service. On your first visit, ask someone in the office to show you the current procedure for making backups, taking detailed notes. Determine whether or not they might benefit from special software and offer to make the trip to the computer store to research their options.

Each time you perform your service, do so with scrupulous care, making absolutely sure you have everything labeled neatly and correctly. Your service, if it's flawless, will be deeply appreciated by the many businesses that will rely on you to safeguard their vital information.

TRICKS OF THE TRADE

Make a logbook for the company with a record of every back-up disk, who created it, and when it was created.

Learn the "restore" function for each system. You may be the only one who knows how to restore lost files, making you that much more valuable.

Suggest to your employer that someone take home the most recent backups. In case of fire or other disaster, information will be in a safe place.

Look everywhere within five feet of your storage place to make sure there are no magnets that could destroy the data.

PARENTAL GUIDANCE SUGGESTED

You may be instrumental in helping your child find customers. Businesses are most likely to hire your child for this duty if they have some personal knowledge of you. Let your friends know what kind of work your child is looking for and encourage them to give his service a try. Leave the cold calling to him and encourage him as he goes about the daunting task of starting a business of this nature. You can provide him with support services, helping him to organize his time and encouraging any opportunity for him to gain knowledge in his field. He will profit more than financially from the time he spends in different office settings and working with different computer and storage systems.

Whether or not you have computer knowledge, keep up enthusiastically with what he is learning and doing. Know that this experience will have a portentous influence on his future.

16

Broker Sawdust and Kindling

WHAT YOU NEED

- advertising fliers
- transportation
- large boxes and bags for collecting
- hacksaw for trimming wood pieces
- smaller boxes and bags for reselling

WHAT TO CHARGE

For sawdust: $2.00 per grocery bagful.
For kindling: $3.50 for a 14″ × 14″ bundle.

FIND THE CUSTOMER

First you need to find the supplier. Sawmills, lumber yards, furniture factories, construction sites—all of these places generate scrap wood. You will have to convince your potential supplier that you are a worthy recipient of their extra lumber. Try doing so by explaining your service and how you plan to be successful at it.

Arrange a regular time to collect and make sure you know just what to take and what not to take. Repackage the kindling, either bundling and tying it with twine or packing it in small boxes you've collected from stores or other sources.

Pack the sawdust in small bags to sell to pet owners or service stations for soaking up oil and gas leaks. Pack it in larger quantities for gardeners' mulch, for spreading on ice on the street or sidewalk, for covering dance floors, or using for decoration at a Western event.

Advertise in the newspaper or "pennysaver" magazine; set up a stand in a well trafficked location or even load up a wagon and go door to door. Try to establish a substantial base of repeat customers. You will save time and money on advertising. Your business should boom during the winter and holiday seasons especially. Be prepared and then enjoy watching your profits roll in.

START HERE

Package your material neatly and be informed as to what kind of wood you are selling and its effectiveness as kindling. Be constantly on the lookout for new and better sources of wood, remembering that successful businesspersons are always looking to improve and innovate. Ask your satisfied customers for referrals and for advice as to how you can better serve them.

If you are able to turn around large quantities of wood, consider contacting community groups (Scouts, schools, church groups) and offer to provide a fund-raising opportunity. You could provide to them the raw material at a lower price; they could do the bundling and selling, thus turning a profit for their group and distributing the product for you.

Print your name on a paper band that encases each bundle or attach a business card to bundles tied with twine. Affix a large sticker to all bags and boxes. Consider adding firestarters. Firestarters are small balls of wax mixed with sawdust, covered with paraffin and tissue paper. They are designed to burn slowly to ignite the larger pieces of wood in the fireplace.

TRICKS OF THE TRADE

Wear gloves. Kindling can have lots of little splinters and the smaller the splinter, the more it hurts. Use paint thinner to remove pitch from your hands. Pine especially is very messy.

If you have trouble with dust making you sneeze or if you have allergies, you may want to invest in some dust masks. A water-soaked bandana wrapped around your face works well too.

Drink more water than you think you need. Hauling wood is an activity that makes you sweat, and dehydration is sneaky.

PARENTAL GUIDANCE SUGGESTED

No doubt you want to avoid turning your backyard into an overgrown wood pile. Help your child establish streamlined methods for storing, packaging, and distributing his wood products supply. Help him to think of effective advertising methods to ensure a quick turnaround of his product. With the high price of kindling in the typical supermarket, your child is in a good position to build a substantial little business.

Support especially his initial efforts and work patiently with him to figure out how best to incorporate the needs of his business into his life and the life of your family.

17
Walk Dogs

WHAT YOU NEED

- ☐ advertising fliers and a phone
- ☐ leash
- ☐ pooper scooper
- ☐ box of dog treats

WHAT TO CHARGE

$1.00 per walk. Consider offering a $.50 discount for a second dog, but only if the dogs are small. (Walking two large dogs is heavy labor!) Ask regular customers to pay you at the end of each week.

FIND THE CUSTOMER

Announce your service with fliers posted on neighborhood bulletin boards; given out at the local pet store,

SPCA, kennel, and pound; posted at the veterinarian's office; and distributed door-to-door.

Whenever you walk dogs, be sure to carry fliers or business cards. Sooner or later, people will walk up to you and say, "What a cute dog you have!" And you can reply, "Thank you. Actually, it's my customer's dog—I have a dog walking service." Then the person may ask for your phone number.

START HERE

Dogs need regular exercise to stay healthy and happy. Unfortunately, their owners can't always give them that exercise; busy schedules, trips out of town, and cold weather can prevent an owner from taking Fido for a walk each day. Here's where you fit in!

The first time you meet with a customer and her dog, find out when, how often, and for how long the owner wants the dog walked. Every day after school for thirty minutes? Every morning for ten minutes?

You'll also need to know where the customer keeps the dog's leash and where the water bowl is. (Dogs drink lots of water after a walk.) If the dog lives indoors and the owner will be gone when you come to walk the dog, you will need to know how to get into the house.

If you get several customers, you may be able to combine your dog walking, taking a few dogs at once. If you do, make sure that the dogs are small and easily managed, and be certain that they get along with each other: you don't want a pack of wild huskies dragging you down the street!

If you like, offer other services with your dog walking. Offer to bathe dogs, clean up dog yards, or water the plants for pet owners who are going out of town for a few days. When your customers know that you're kind, reliable, and honest, they'll hire you for all sorts of jobs.

TRICKS OF THE TRADE

To most folks, the family dog is a precious member of the household. Treat these family members with respect:

- Praise dogs for doing right.
- Never let a dog off its leash on a busy street.
- Reward and discipline dogs consistently. Like people, dogs get confused when your praise and punishment is always changing.
- Clean up dog messes so others don't have to.
- Don't ride a bicycle while holding a dog by the leash; if the dog bolts to chase a cat, it will pull you off the bike.
- Give dogs plenty of water. They don't have sweat glands, so they cool down by drinking water and panting.

PARENTAL GUIDANCE SUGGESTED

As always, know where your child's customers live; accompany him there for his first appointments. Join him on his first walks and help him map out a walking route that's safe for him and the dogs. Choosing a route is an important task. It requires looking through the eyes of someone else to determine what's best for that person, or in this case, what's best for that animal.

If your child walks several different dogs, ask him to describe the personalities of each one. There are probably some dramatic differences. Talk about what those differences are and what causes one animal to behave differently from another. Undoubtedly, some of the dogs have been overdisciplined, some underdisciplined, some spoiled, some neglected. Help your child learn by this simple example how environment dramatically affects behavior—for both animals and humans.

18

Clean Vacant Homes

Independent, self-motivated young person needed to clean newly constructed or recently vacated homes in preparation for new occupants.

WHAT YOU NEED

- advertising fliers
- vacuum cleaner (bring along extra bags)
- rags and sponges
- rubber gloves (surgical gloves work well and are cheap)
- glass cleaner
- all-purpose cleaner
- spackle and putty knife
- toilet paper (in case you need to use the bathroom. . . . good thinking, eh?)

WHAT TO CHARGE

$5.00 to $7.00 per hour.

FIND THE CUSTOMER

Contact every contractor you can. Present each one with a flier that lists all the things you can clean. Bring along a letter of reference from a previous customer as soon as you get one. Offer a free trial cleaning. Do the same thing for every realty office in your town. Ask the real estate agents to include your flier in the paperwork for people who are buying, selling, or renting a home. All of them can use your service. Go to large apartment complexes and talk to the manager. Tell her you will do a great job and save her time and money. Prove it in your free trial cleaning.

START HERE

Meet the contractor, Realtor, apartment manager, homeowner—whoever employs you—at the house you will be cleaning. Make a very specific list of what you're to do and ask the person to sign it. Your agreement will be clearly spelled out, and no one will be able to argue about whether you did what you were told. Get the keys and agree on the time you will come back to do the job.

When you come back to clean, unload your equipment and lock yourself in the house. It is unlikely that you will be in any danger, but every now and then people go into unoccupied homes when they don't belong there. You will feel safer with the door locked.

Do the bathroom cleaning first, wearing rubber gloves. Then, if the house has been previously occupied, find nail holes in the wall and fill them with spackling paste. Then clean the kitchen counters, appliances, mirrors, and windows. Last, sweep and mop the floors.

Walk through a few times, looking through the eyes of your employer. See if there's anything you might have missed. Check your list twice.

Go back to your employer and present the checklist as your bill. Make sure you get paid on the spot.

TRICKS OF THE TRADE

You may want a teammate for this job. If you join up with a friend, you will have to convince your potential customers that both of you are serious about working. They don't want kids using a new home for a football field while no one's watching. Be professional. Dress nicely when you meet with potential clients and include in your flier any information that might help persuade someone that you can be wholly trusted.

Play music on the job. It will help keep your energy up. Use care in your choice of music. Employers who hear acid rock wailing away while you work will wonder if they made the right decision in hiring you. Fair or not, that's the way it works. You might want to consider bringing books on tape or stories like "Adventures in Odyssey" from Focus on the Family. You'll be amazed at how quickly the time passes as you work and listen to an exciting story.

PARENTAL GUIDANCE SUGGESTED

Don't hesitate to closely monitor your child's safety. Know exactly where she is and who is employing her. Consider providing her with a portable phone. That way you will always be able to contact her, and she can contact you. Though expensive, a portable phone can be a lifeline to young kids and teenagers in many situations. You will find it a worthwhile investment.

Help her analyze and organize her supplies. Make sure she is using effective and safe products. Because she will be exposed to substantial amounts of a cleaning solution, make sure the solution is safe. Better a little more expense now than potentially tragic health problems later.

Encourage her success by providing some convenience

items she might not think about getting for herself. You might buy a colorful plastic bin or an inexpensive rolling cart for her supplies. You might get a plastic case for her fliers so that they don't get wet. Though it is not necessary to buy a lot of things, buying a few helpful items is one way to show your enthusiastic support of her venture.

Pay attention to her records to make sure that she is making enough money for the time and expense involved. Strategize with her about ways that she can work faster while still maintaining high quality.

Enjoy watching her develop a multitude of skills: communication skills, organization skills, and efficient cleaning techniques. She will use them the rest of her life.

19

Iron Clothes

Neat, wrinkle-free person needed to iron for busy clients with heaps of wrinkle-infested clothing.

WHAT YOU NEED

- advertising fliers and/or business cards
- a reliable iron and ironing board
- spray bottles of water and starch

WHAT TO CHARGE

$1.00 per item of clothing or $5.00 to $7.00 per hour.

FIND THE CUSTOMER

Many adults of today grew up in the era of polyester and wash-and-wear, and they happily considered the task of ironing a relic of the past. Now, with the popularity of natural fibers, that tedious but satisfying chore has crept back into our busy lives. Consider targeting your advertising to young adults who live in the fast lane and wouldn't be caught dead in anything but all-cotton clothing. They've got the need, but they haven't got the time.

Post your fliers at a local health club, at day-care centers, at health food stores, and at your school and other schools, both private and public, in your area.

Take your business cards to the mall and ask store owners, especially those who deal in cotton clothing, if you may leave a supply of the cards on their counters. Advertise as well among the elderly or infirm.

START HERE

Get some training in ironing from an expert. That could be your mom! If not, ask your friends' moms or grandmoms—eventually you'll find someone who knows the particulars of this special skill. It's important that you are good at what you do, especially when you deal with clothing that may be very expensive.

Consider offering a pick-up and delivery service to your clients for a small service charge. You might pick up at the client's home or place of business and return there as well. That way you can do your work in your own home with your familiar and dependable equipment.

Attach a business card or two to every delivery, politely asking your customer to pass it along to a friend or colleague if he is pleased with your service.

If you build a small base of customers whom you continue to please, you will find that with repeat business and referrals, your venture will flourish. Consistency and quality work are the key to success in this enterprise. Your customers will inevitably find your service indispensable.

TRICKS OF THE TRADE

Keep your iron and ironing board extremely clean to avoid any transfer of dirt or stain.

If you accidentally scorch a garment, sponge it with a piece of cotton which has been soaked in a 3 percent peroxide solution. For clothes made of linen and cotton, dampen a cloth with the peroxide, lay it on the scorched area, and iron with a warm iron.

Be scrupulously careful about keeping your customers' clothing organized. Perhaps you can label each garment with a string tag wrapped around a button.

Treat your clients' clothing with great respect, always doing your very best work on each piece.

PARENTAL GUIDANCE SUGGESTED

There is great value in learning to treat others' possessions with respect. If we all learned it, we might avoid a few wars, famines, and the like. Make sure your child receives thorough training so that she can be confident and take pride in her skill. She must know how to handle a whole range of fabrics. The resulting knowledge of textiles will stand her in good stead in other ways as well.

Help her figure out a workable collection and distribution system. If she doesn't yet drive, you may be her business partner for this function. Though it may seem a tedious waste of time for you to haul other people's laundry around town, it may, in fact, be a wonderful opportunity for you to share time and experience with your child.

Let her know that her work has value, both to herself and to her customers. Perhaps you could encourage her to listen to quality story tapes as she irons, doubling the value of her time.

Never forget to notice and express your pleasure in a job well done.

20
Wrap Gifts

Creative, dextrous worker needed to pack
and wrap stacks of gifts for the holidays.

WHAT YOU NEED

- advertising fliers and business cards
- wrapping paper
- boxes
- scissors
- tape
- ribbons
- tags
- pens
- postage scale and packaging supplies (optional)

WHAT TO CHARGE

$3.50 per gift for wrapping only.
$7.00 for wrapping and mailing; add postage to your fee.

FIND THE CUSTOMER

Print creative fliers that potential customers can pull out of a beautifully wrapped box. Ask local merchants to display them. Put them at craft fairs, gift shops, bookstores—any place that does not do its own wrapping. Ask to display at the post office or other mailing centers that do not offer competing services. Distribute your fliers at school and church as well.

START HERE

You can run this business from your home, with customers dropping off their packages at your house to be wrapped and/or mailed. You can also set up a booth at a local shopping mall (with the mall's permission) and catch shoppers right there. Be sure to check the prices of any competitors at the mall and charge accordingly. Also be sure that your fliers have preceded you in the community and in the mall.

Offer an array of gift wrap designs, appropriate for different ages and sexes. Display them by wrapping empty boxes.

Obviously, this business is mostly seasonal but not entirely. While Christmas will be your busiest time, requiring long hours and an intensive commitment, don't forget Mother's Day, Father's Day, and Valentine's Day. Take advantage of the wedding season as well. You can design your fliers according to the upcoming season, circulating them two to three weeks ahead of time (even earlier for Christmas gift wrapping).

If customers are dropping off gifts to be wrapped and mailed, be sure you have a foolproof system to keep them properly identified. You don't want Aunt Agnes receiving the stuffed dinosaur and little Billy getting the dried fruit arrangement. Have each customer fill out a special tag with the gift recipient's name, address, age, and sex.

Gift giving in our culture can be a wearisome and annoying task. Many of your customers will be in a frenzy, panicking about all they have to accomplish in too little time. You have an opportunity to change an angry shopper's attitude by your sweet and helpful spirit, by your efficiency and respect for their time, and simply by your sincere desire to provide them a service, in the best sense of the word.

TRICKS OF THE TRADE

Buy your seasonal wrapping *after* each holiday. You can buy at half price or less and save it all until the next year.

Take a gift wrapping class at a store or through an adult education course. You can learn some techniques for creating stunning packages, and creativity will be a strong selling point in your business. If you can create something your customer cannot, you have a great advantage.

Attach a business card to each wrapped gift. You will expand your customer base.

PARENTAL GUIDANCE SUGGESTED

Gift wrapping, even at Christmas, can be an enjoyable experience. Help your child make the most of this business by supporting him in his efforts to acquire skill. Work with him in finding the best wraps and ribbons and watch for classes or workshops where he can learn spectacular wraps. Encourage his creativity; help him go the extra mile in making his customer's gifts special and unique.

Getting the word out around the community can be challenging in a venture like this. Brainstorm with your child, coming up with advertising ideas—from the mundane to the ridiculous. Let him feel your support and abiding interest in his success.

21
Fix Bicycles

> Reliable, mechanically inclined person needed to fix flats, adjust brakes, lubricate, and tune gears of neglected bicycles.

WHAT YOU NEED

- ☐ advertising fliers
- ☐ bike tools
- ☐ patch kit
- ☐ lubricant
- ☐ rags

WHAT TO CHARGE

$8.00 to $10.00 per hour, plus parts.

FIND THE CUSTOMER

Competitive cyclists and triathletes with high-end equipment will look toward professional mechanics to service their bikes. Your friends and neighbors, however, who use their bikes for curb jumping and getting to school, need *you*.

Advertise at schools, your own and others, and in the PTA newsletter so students and parents hear about you as well. Hand out fliers around the neighborhood that include endorsements of your skill from other customers and even from the local bike shop owner. Blitz the neighborhood after Christmas with a tune-up special for new bikes and old. Post your eye-catching fliers on bulletin boards at local parks and health clubs. If your town has holiday parades, walk along the parade route passing out fliers and shaking hands. Bring some candy to hand to the youngsters.

Hang signs on your bike and on your friends' bikes that boldly advertise your business name and phone number. Ride around town.

START HERE

Obviously you need to acquire some repair and adjustment skills to be successful. If you have access to a bike expert, ask for lessons. Buy books on bike repair. *Anybody's Bike Book* by Tom Cuthbertson makes bike repair easy and fun. Hang around the bike shop with a list of questions to ask. Get knowledge any way you can, then practice it on your own bike and anybody else's who's willing.

Decide which repairs you want to offer in your service. If you limit yourself to common repairs that you have already mastered, you'll find it easier to keep a consistent and steady pace of business going. As time goes by and business goes well, you can start offering more exotic services; but at first, keep it simple.

When your customer delivers (or you pick up) a bike, give her an estimate of the time it will take to repair it and what the cost will be. Tell her that if it takes longer than you anticipate or requires new parts that you will call her.

Be sure you do. Because you're young, you will have to be extra diligent in order to earn your customer's trust.

Note the date of repair on your calendar, then write your customer's name and phone number on the date two weeks forward. On that day, give your customer a call and ask if the bike has been performing to the customer's satisfaction. If not, offer to look at the bike again. If so, politely ask your customer to pass your name on to a friend so that your business can grow.

TRICKS OF THE TRADE

Consider writing a proposal asking your school administration, student council, and PTA to allow you to open and run a bike repair shop on your school campus. Provide your service before and after school and run your business for school credit. Submit a business plan that includes hiring qualified and trustworthy students as the shop grows. You could pilot a dynamite new program wherein students learn business by doing business right at school. You may be challenged by security concerns, insurance considerations, supervision issues and such, but it's worth a shot. Who knows, you could start an education revolution by your example of initiative and enterprise. Give it a whirl!

Invest in a good set of tools. Consider asking a parent or grandparent to invest in your business by helping you buy the right equipment and tools. Be sure to draw up a contract that specifies how and when you will pay your investor back—with interest.

Keep a card file with each customer's name, address, and a quick description of the repair or service. If you solve a certain problem then encounter it again, you will have it written down in your files and will be able to refer to it easily. Also, if a customer complains, your card file might be a helpful source of information as it will be a description of what you did, when you did it, and why.

Develop a relationship with a local bike shop. Even though you are in competition, you also can be an asset to the shop when you order parts and make referrals. Let the bike shop owner or manager know that if he can help you, you will buy all your parts there and send others as well.

PARENTAL GUIDANCE SUGGESTED

Bike lovers can make good money in the bike repair business. Chances are, if you have a mechanically-minded child who loves to hide away and tinker, you also have a child who is not particularly extroverted. This is not always the case, but if it is in your house, you will need to provide extra support in the area of customer relations. The last thing your child may want to do is call some potentially intimidating adult and tell him that the part's on backorder or that the bike ought to be sold for scrap metal or that the repair is more costly than he originally thought. You can help your child by encouraging his responsibility in this area. Lighten the load by offering to rent a movie as soon as the phone calls are made or standing ready to pop a piece of candy in his mouth every time he finishes a call. Let him know it's not so bad and assure him that he'll get used to it some day.

Lend a listening ear to tales of frustration, speaking of your confidence in his ability to solve problems and overcome hurdles. Standing in the garage now and then and watching quietly provides some of the best support you can offer.

22

Be a Butler

Courteous, hard-working servant needed to assist hostess at parties and large gatherings.

WHAT YOU NEED

- advertising fliers
- impeccable manners
- appropriate clothing (probably a tuxedo-like outfit)

WHAT TO CHARGE

$5.00 per hour.

FIND THE CUSTOMER

Once again, word of mouth is your best source of advertising. Your reputation will both precede you and follow you. Make sure that you guard it carefully.

Distribute your fliers door to door, in front of party supply stores, and at grocery stores (with permission). Wear your best butler attire—a suit and tie for boys and a formal dress for girls, or better yet, a tailored tuxedo for either sex. If possible, serve your potential customer a fruit drink or some hors d'oeuvres and then present to him a flier with a flourish.

Let him know that you are responsible and polite and, if you can, offer the name and phone number of a previous customer willing to give you a good reference. Be sure to speak pleasantly and confidently, looking your customer in the eye.

Coordinate your advertising with the appropriate upcoming holiday attire. If you're advertising before St. Patrick's Day, wear a green carnation as a boutonniere. Before Christmas, wear a red bow tie and cummerbund. Before Valentine's Day, suggest to your potential customer that you serve a romantic dinner for two at a park or the beach. Parties big and small can be enhanced by your service.

Don't forget to target children's birthday parties. Advertise to preschools, elementary schools, play groups, and mothers' support groups. You can be of enormous help to parents.

START HERE

When you are hired, find out from the host how he would prefer you to dress and how much time before and after the party you should plan to stay. Be aware that parties often last longer than planned.

It is very important for you to be willing to perform whatever task necessary to assist the party-giver. Vacuuming the floor, washing dishes, and even watching young children before and during the party all fall under your job description. While serving food and drink is certainly the job of a butler, you may be called upon to do any number of things. It's important that you be flexible and enthusiastically helpful in whatever capacity your host or hostess requires.

Take initiative. Your employer will have plenty more to do than to direct your every task. If the punch bowl looks empty, fill it. If the table needs clearing, clear it. If dishes are dirty, wash them. There's no end to what you can find to do if you only look around with eyes to see it all. Nothing will impress the party-giver more than your self-directed help.

Before you agree to work, politely explain to the host or hostess that it is against the law for you to work where alcohol is being served. Working only at parties free of alcohol will reduce your customer base, but it will also reduce your exposure to the dangers associated with drinking and will keep you in compliance with important labor laws.

Be aware of and able to deal with any threatening or irresponsible actions from the adults around you. Drinking or not, sometimes grown-ups make disappointing behavior choices. If someone is treating you in a way that makes you feel uncomfortable, talk to your host or hostess and leave the party. Your safety and dignity are worth far more than the job.

Being a butler or server at a party can be an enjoyable experience. Providing truly helpful service, interacting warmly and politely with guests, taking initiative to solve problems and do chores before being asked—it's a satisfying way to make money, because your job well done will, more often than not, make you friends as well. Knock yourself out to do the best job you can do, and you will undoubtedly become the richest and most sought after butler in town!

TRICKS OF THE TRADE

Read books written by Thornton Wilder, Henry James, or Edith Wharton—books set in a time when life seemed to revolve around people's manners. They're great stories, and you'll be amazed at what you learn about politeness and decorum.

Learn a few simple magic tricks and save them for the right moment. If the kids at the party are getting rowdy, show off a few tricks to quiet them down and wow your employer.

At cleanup time, wear an apron printed with the name of your company. Keep extra fliers or business cards in your pocket to pass on to any interested party guests.

Never gossip about who or what you've seen at someone's party. Tempting as it may be to share juicy information with your friends, it is not only unprofessional but just plain wrong.

PARENTAL GUIDANCE SUGGESTED

Your role in this job is twofold. The first part is easy. Teach your child superior manners. Teach him how to address adults, how to greet someone politely, how to hold a pleasant conversation. Teach him to take initiative, to be humble yet confident, to be bright yet respectful. Teach him basic cooking and cleaning skills. Teach him to clean up after himself. OK, so the first part isn't so easy. It might take an entire lifetime to accomplish.

The second part is not easy either. You must be your child's protector as best you can. While being a butler seems like a harmless enough job, in this day and age, it has its risks. Your child may be in the home of near strangers whose behavior you cannot see or control. You never know what may go on. Teach your child to know when he is in danger and what to do. Teach him to trust his feelings and to act when he feels threatened or uncomfortable with his surroundings. Every time he works, be available to pick him up if necessary, always letting him know that his safety and security are of utmost importance.

Do not allow your child to work at a party where there will be alcohol served. It is illegal and can significantly increase risks to your child's safety.

With good supervision and honest communication, your child will gain valuable experience and a chance to build character through service.

23
Set Out Garbage Cans

Energetic, agreeable person needed to work once a week dragging garbage cans to curb for pick-up, later returning them to customer's house.

WHAT YOU NEED

☐ advertising fliers   ☐ gloves

WHAT TO CHARGE

$1.00 per can per week. For $.50 extra, replace the trash can liner. Once a month offer a can cleaning service for $1.00 a can.

FIND THE CUSTOMER

Your neighborhood is the place to start. Present yourself and your fliers door to door, offering a free trial week. You might list on your flier three or four ways that you've proven yourself to be reliable. Add a quote from a teacher or friend about your cheerful attitude.

Tell your potential customer that, while you want to make money and learn something about business, you also want to contribute something to the neighborhood. Chances are, many of your neighbors will give your service a try.

START HERE

After you've made the sale, ask your customer to show you where he stores his cans and where on the curb he would like you to put them on pick-up day. Write this information in a notebook. This will not only impress your client, it will help you to remember these details when the time comes.

On the appointed day, be prompt. You probably can take the cans to the curb before school and return them after school. Be sure to place the cans and lids neatly where they belong, and you will win your customers' hearts in no time.

To collect your fee, just decide on a day (the first Saturday of the month, for instance) and go to each house with a smile and a thank you. Ask your customers if there is any way you can improve your service. Tell them you appreciate their business.

As time permits, you may opt to branch out, covering other neighborhoods whose trash service falls on a different day.

TRICKS OF THE TRADE

The number of your customers will grow along with your reputation. Here's how to grow a reputation:

- Always be on time.
- Move quickly and efficiently.
- Pick up any trash that has fallen behind the cans and

any that spills to the ground when the can is emptied into the garbage truck.

- Respect your customers' property: Don't walk on her fence or throw rocks from his rock garden onto the street.
- Greet customers by name.
- Give your customers a candy heart for Valentine's Day, a small pumpkin for Halloween, a Christmas card for the holidays.

PARENTAL GUIDANCE SUGGESTED

Though this job seems to require little skill, it is, in fact, a great exercise in public relations. Salesmanship is a key requisite, and you can assist your child in developing an array of appropriate skills. Basic courtesy, listening skills, and people-pleasing small talk is as crucial to garbage-can moving as it is to a presidential election. These qualities will help your child establish a successful money-making enterprise.

24

Deliver Muffins and Juice

Cheerful, early-rising baker needed to make fresh muffins and juice for weekly delivery through the neighborhood.

WHAT YOU NEED

- advertising fliers or menus
- recipes
- muffin pans
- inexpensive plastic pitchers
- an electric juicer (optional)

WHAT TO CHARGE

$2.50 for a half dozen muffins; $3.75 for a half gallon of fresh squeezed juice; $2.75 for your special mix of frozen fruit juices.

FIND THE CUSTOMER

Pick a sunny Saturday morning. Bake a basketful of muffins, fill a jug with juice, and start walking. Go house to house, quickly explaining your service. Offer each person a free muffin and a paper cup of juice, leaving a flier behind.

Your flier can include a short menu and an order form that customers can drop by your house or mail to you. If they ordered your service, ask at what time they would like to enjoy their muffins and juice. You might ask what their favorite muffins are and add that flavor to your menu.

Be sure to offer low-fat or no-sugar muffins and let your customers know about the health benefits of your muffins over store-bought varieties. You might bring along a package of store-bought muffins and compare prices and ingredients, proving to your potential customer that your fresh-baked goods are far superior to any alternative. When it comes time to deliver, remember that a big smile, a polite and enthusiastic greeting, and maybe even the morning paper picked up from the driveway will make your muffins taste even better—and will keep your orders coming.

START HERE

Besides your appealing personality, superior manners, creative presentation, and responsible service, your menu is a key factor to your success. Spend time researching your options. Experiment with recipes both basic and exotic.

Think up creative names for your juices and muffins, perhaps using references to local people and places. Trim your printed menu in the shape of a big muffin.

Your resourcefulness and unique manner of service will speak volumes to your customers, making them feel pampered and special. Needless to say, your business will grow as a result and so will the deep satisfaction of knowing that you are bringing sunshine into the lives of each person you serve.

TRICKS OF THE TRADE

Your early-morning service can help customers get their day off to a great start. Here's how to do this in style:

- Find out customers' birthdays and deliver muffins with candles. If you're brave you can even sing to them!
- If a customer has company, provide the guest with a free muffin and juice.
- Decorate your muffins according to the season. A simple sprig of holly, a red doily, a few candy corns—these extras cost little and add much.
- Pass out free samples when you're introducing a new recipe.
- Rarely would you need a permit for this endeavor, but call the county health department to check. Ask what you should know to make sure your products are safe and healthy. Be sure to follow any guidelines you're given.

PARENTAL GUIDANCE SUGGESTED

This is a job particularly suited for that special brand of kid who loves to make friends. Encourage creativity, perhaps finding out the birthdays of your neighbors and presenting muffins accordingly.

How about helping your child set up a system whereby neighbors buy muffins for each other? That way the Harrises would be buying for the Snyders and the Snyders would buy for the Kings, the Kings would buy for the Harrises, etc., etc. Think how much fun the neighborhood could have on muffins alone.

Help your child see the enormous value in binding a neighborhood together and in building a tighter, more affectionate community.

25

Bake Bread

Baker of fine, warm, healthy bread needed to make and distribute it throughout the neighborhood, perhaps beyond. Must be able to think ahead, cheerful, and accommodating.

WHAT YOU NEED

- advertising fliers
- automatic bread machine
- recipe books
- personalized bread bags (available in the Miles Kimball gift catalog; send request for free catalog to 41 W. Eighth Ave., Oshkosh, WI 54901)

WHAT TO CHARGE

$1.00 per loaf; $2.00 for dinner rolls, braided loaves, pizza crust—anything you have to reshape and cook in the oven.

FIND THE CUSTOMER

An easy sell! Make a variety of healthy breads and rolls and head down the block. Offer your potential customer a slice of his choice and a flier explaining the multiple advantages of eating homemade bread. It's healthier, cheaper, and a whole lot tastier! Offer to supply your neighbor with a fresh loaf every day, every other day, or whatever frequency he prefers. Tell him the bread will always be delivered fresh!

START HERE

Get to know your recipes and your bread making machine. Figure out how many loaves you can produce in your available time. Your bread machine will do most of the work, but you will have to organize a schedule of production. Deliver your loaves in personalized bread bags so that your customer will be reminded everyday of your terrific service.

TRICKS OF THE TRADE

- Deliver your bread while it's warm. Warm bread seems to go with warm hearts.
- Include a treat now and then. Throw in a cinnamon roll or a muffin or a slice of something exotic.
- Thank your customers often for using your service.
- Learn and use your customers' names whenever you greet them.

PARENTAL GUIDANCE SUGGESTED

Chances are it will be your bread machine that produces these luscious loaves. Consider renting it to your young entrepreneur or starting a savings program to buy another machine to be used solely for business purposes. Working with your child in this way will provide invaluable lessons in good business practice and in good household management. You and your child can figure out the cost of different types of bread. You can figure out what is saved in time and money by buying supplies in bulk. You can show her how to keep simple but thorough records. Take pride in being the one to train your child in these crucial skills that will benefit her for life.

26

Cut Coupons

Newspaper buff needed to cut and sort coupons on a weekly basis. Must be diligent and attentive to detail.

WHAT YOU NEED

- ☐ advertising fliers
- ☐ envelopes
- ☐ good pair of scissors (your customers provide the newspapers)

WHAT TO CHARGE

$2.00 per family per week.

FIND THE CUSTOMER

Head out to the neighborhood, fliers in hand, to tell your neighbors that they no longer need to spend their precious time cutting coupons because there is an enterprising kid standing ready to do it for them. Tell them you can cut and organize their coupons, sorting them and placing them in customized envelopes for delivery.

Tell them that, because you will have multiple customers, you will have multiple coupon sources. Everyone will benefit as you suit your categories to each customer. For instance, if aged Mrs. Jones gives you her paper, you can use the diaper coupons you find there for the Williams family who have twin babies. Mrs. Jones may benefit from the medicine coupons that the Williams family doesn't need, and so on.

Make up a sample grocery list to include in your flier. Show your potential customers that if they shop with coupons (and double coupons) they can save about $10.00 per $100.00 of groceries each week. Your service will provide them a net savings of $8.00 each week—with no time investment for them whatsoever! You will simply deliver their coupons, cut and sorted into labeled envelopes, and off they will go to the store. Everybody wins!

START HERE

Ask your customer to save the daily paper for you. Each week, on an appointed day, pick up the week's supply of papers and give to your customer the previous week's coupons, cut and sorted into prearranged categories. Be sure to keep a notebook with a record of where each customer shops so you can catch any specials or double coupons.

If you can build your customer base to ten families, you will spend about five hours a week with their newspapers, cutting, sorting, and delivering. If each family pays you $2.00 per week you will net $80.00 a month in your business!

TRICKS OF THE TRADE

Here's how to impress your customers with the quality and convenience of your service:

- *Presentation:* Clip neatly and use nice envelopes. A little neatness goes a long way.
- *Communication:* Ask your customers how you're doing —and how you might improve your service to be more helpful to them.
- *Politeness:* Show your customers that you consider it a privilege to help families in this way!

PARENTAL GUIDANCE SUGGESTED

This is your opportunity to further instruct your child in the lost art of thrift. He will quickly learn the value of wise shopping—that thoughtful planning and careful purchasing is a worthy pursuit. Learning that lesson now could work dramatically in your child's favor as he grows up in our wasteful, impulse-oriented culture. Though his job as neighborhood coupon cutter can become tiresome, he can learn, with your strong support, that his contribution is ongoing and of sure value to his customers.

You can help him figure out how to organize the coupons. You can buy him a plastic file holder for his envelope supply. You can protect him from interference from younger children in the family. By treating his business seriously, you will help him stay motivated.

Encourage your neighbors, if you are well acquainted, to let your child know how his service is helping the family both financially and organizationally. One family keeps their coupon savings in a special container and uses it to sponsor a needy child. Another gives it to a specific missions organization that provides food for the hungry. Another family may save it for a special vacation. It would be nice for your child to know these things, and he might even venture to suggest an idea of this sort to the customers himself.

Applaud his efforts, his careful cutting, his neatly arranged piles, the polite manner in which he communicates. Note any area of growth in skill or maturity and comment on it, helping your child see that his chosen responsibility has great value and he deserves to be proud of his accomplishment.

27

Organize Shows

Pied piper with interest in the arts needed to organize neighborhood, church, or school performances. Must be able to communicate an enthusiasm for the art of public speaking and inspire younger kids to participate in memorizing and presenting great works of literature.

WHAT YOU NEED

☐ skills listed above   ☐ business cards

WHAT TO CHARGE

You provide a free service to the kids involved in the performance, but charge admission for the audience. Parents won't mind paying to see the show, especially when it is good! Plan on charging $3.00 per person. Let kids under 5 watch for free.

FIND THE CUSTOMER

People of all ages benefit enormously from the experience of performance, yet children are far more often in the audience than they are on the stage. A few generations ago, families would gather together to hear their children's "elocution exercises": poems and stories that kids memorized and recited in front of small audiences.

Not only did these gatherings give kids solid experience in public speaking, they also required memorizing excerpts of great literature, which the children often remembered for a lifetime. Consider reviving this valuable tradition in your neighborhood, church, or school.

Include in your show displays of other skills: dance, instrumental music, and the like. Parents will appreciate the educational experience for their kids; kids will enjoy and benefit from the opportunity; you will make some money and provide a valuable service to your community.

Contact neighborhood parents, school officials, and church personnel with a personal letter explaining what you are planning and why. Be honest about how you intend to make some money but stress the value of your venture to the participants.

Ask for a meeting to discuss where and when you might carry out your plan. Follow up with a phone call and make an appointment to meet. Bring a sample selection of material—exciting poems, short dramatic sketches, songs, and stories. Explain how you will work with the children and what your goals are for their performance. Arrange a time, place, and date for rehearsals and show.

START HERE

After selling your innovative idea to parents, school officials, or church leaders, you need to sell it to the kids. You can. If you are excited about the value of learning high-quality material, they will be also.

Work with each child, as schedules permit, for about two weeks, encouraging confident presentation, clear diction, and dramatic intensity.

Set your standards high, demanding excellence in an atmosphere of encouragement. You'll be amazed at what those kids will do. If your program is well received, you can hold it on a quarterly basis using the same kids and different material.

Arrange to hold your show either in an appropriately large home, in a church, or in some other workable location. Enthusiastic kids can make and deliver invitations and might even provide refreshments. After one successful show, ask a parent or administrator to write a recommendation of your program. Include it in your next round of letters.

In a short time you will prove yourself, and your good reputation will spread quickly. In an era when excellence in the arts is increasingly scarce and school programs have all but disappeared, your business will provide a significant service to your community and quite possibly a life-changing opportunity for a talented child.

TRICKS OF THE TRADE

Contact the local newspaper and TV news. Let them know that you are involved in an innovative and challenging educational experience for the children of the community. You may find yourself on the front page.

Make sure your literary selections have artistic merit. They can be entertaining and fun but should also be of excellent quality.

Show kids the video of *Anne of Avonlea*. There is an engaging "elocution" scene that the kids may enjoy.

It is unlikely that, for your purposes, you would have to

pay royalties on the material presented in your show. Nonetheless, you should call the publisher of the book from which you got the selection and ask permission to perform it.

PARENTAL GUIDANCE SUGGESTED

This unorthodox method of business carries some initial risk and frustration as your child must establish trust and gain the active support of busy adults. Stand behind your youngster in this initial phase because success will be sweet. Help him with creative problem-solving, especially in finding appealing ways to motivate his young charges to pursue true excellence.

His job will be challenging, but remind him that things worthwhile always are. Continually support his efforts as he makes a singularly valuable contribution to the lives of children with whom he is working. He is a coach—a coach of the mind—whose impact will be long remembered and appreciated by many. Laborious details, uncooperative kids or adults, even apparent failure should be viewed only from the larger perspective that you can provide. The initiative required for a service of this nature should be itself a source of pride for you both.

28

Sweep Patios and Garages

WHAT YOU NEED

- advertising fliers and a phone
- notebook
- a regular broom
- a push broom
- a dust pan
- a well-fitting pair of work gloves
- a portable stereo to put rhythm in your strokes (optional)

WHAT TO CHARGE

$3.00 for the garage or the patio, $5.00 for both.

FIND THE CUSTOMER

Take a walk through the neighborhood, offering a free sample of your work. Let your customer choose garage or patio. Let him know that you can provide this service every week and can even make arrangements to sweep before company comes. Tell your customer that you are efficient and energetic and will work hard to meet your mutual high standards.

If he doesn't hire you right then and there, leave him with a flier and thank him for the opportunity to have been of service. If he does hire you, agree on a regular schedule and write it down in a notebook along with his name, address, and phone number.

START HERE

When you arrive at the house, knock at the door to let your customer know you are there. After a polite greeting, go to work. Your customer will be watching to see if you are fast and thorough.

Use a standard broom to sweep in corners. Sweep from the walls and ceiling any cobwebs you can reach with the broom. The push broom will work well for the large, open areas. When you have swept the dirt and leaves into a neat pile, use the dust pan to dispose of it carefully into the trash.

Your energy and determination will keep your customers satisfied, and as the word spreads throughout the neighborhood, you and your service will be in demand.

TRICKS OF THE TRADE

Always be on time. Your customer will be very impressed.

If you bring a tape player or radio, be sure to wear headphones. Keep the volume low so that you can hear if the customer calls to you.

Think of extra things you can do, just to help out. For instance, one day bring a can of glass cleaner and clean the window in the garage. Offer to hose off the driveway—

free of charge—just to be generous, no other reason. Your customer will not only be impressed, he'll be surprised!

PARENTAL GUIDANCE SUGGESTED

Kids who are physically active, who are self-directed, and who love to be outdoors are likely to succeed at this job. Provide your child with on-the-job training, instructing him how to do his job effectively and efficiently. Consider buying him high-quality brooms to let him know you are taking his work seriously.

Provide extra incentives, special events, and privileges as a reward for his good work. Now and then surprise him on the job with a tall glass of his favorite drink or freshly baked cookies.

As your child finds customers and settles into a routine, continually encourage him, expressing appreciation for the service he is providing to the neighbors. Let him know that he is surely contributing to his customers' lives by taking over a tiring chore. Though you can express satisfaction in his good work, it's best to elicit his own response. Ask him how he feels about his work. Help him to identify and be aware of his own good feelings of satisfaction in his efforts.

Encourage him to show appreciation for his customers' business by helping him make for them occasional treats, seasonal cards, and other tokens of appreciation. Though he will enjoy his spending money, his growth will come largely from the gift of service he is giving to those around him. Help him recognize the value of building friendships through courtesy and dependability.

29
Pay Bills

WHAT YOU NEED

- business cards or advertising fliers
- calculator with tape printer

WHAT TO CHARGE

$7.00 per hour.

FIND THE CUSTOMER

Run an ad in your local paper that says something like this: "Need time to organize your paperwork, clean up your files, prepare your bills? Let an honest, reliable young entrepreneur do it for you. Call Kim Thompson at 555-0123."

Ask your adult friends and relatives to think of people they know who might be able to use your service. Ideally, your adult friend can recommend you, then pave the way for an introduction.

Although just about any adult can use this service, it will especially appeal to the very wealthy, who have a particular load of paperwork, and to single parents, who have a particular lack of time. People who travel a lot, who are in the performing or visual arts, or who are very active socially also tend to need this type of help.

START HERE

Many of the details of this job will be worked out between you and your client, according to his needs. Your client may be organized but busy and may already have a system in place that you simply operate. Or your client may be helplessly disorganized and need you to design systems to control the flow of paperwork and bring order to his whole life.

You may be asked to file, fill out checks, balance a checkbook, RSVP invitations, help prepare tax returns, or other office tasks.

You may copy and file recipes, organize photo albums, drop off dry cleaning, get film developed, return phone calls, order from catalogs, put together scrapbooks, or buy and send gifts. In fact, you may simply be shown a messy desk and asked to dive in, in whatever way you can! So much depends on the needs and personality of your client.

Obviously, you must be flexible, willing to tailor your services to each situation differently. You must be a good communicator, willing to ask questions and able to remember answers.

TRICKS OF THE TRADE

Confidentiality is a key trait in a personal assistant. No one should know your client's personal business. Sharing information about your employer is an unthinkable breach of trust.

Be ever accurate. Check your numbers, then recheck your numbers. Paying bills, balancing a checkbook—they're quite a responsibility. Take it seriously.

Act like a professional. You are. Call your employer Mr. or Mrs. unless directed otherwise. Use impeccable phone manners, remembering that everything you say reflects upon your employer. Write neatly and precisely.

Even though you and your employer become friends, you must never forget that you are in a position of service. Continue behaving professionally even after you get to know him. Your employer will respect you for doing so, and you will respect yourself.

PARENTAL GUIDANCE SUGGESTED

Your child can gain important experience simply by seeing intimately how another person lives. She will also gain skill as she attends to various tasks, all of which she will do for herself as an adult.

If she has difficulty communicating with her client, make sure you enable her to solve the problem, resisting the temptation to do it for her, especially if the client is a friend of yours. On the other hand, if you feel that she is in danger for some reason or is being taken advantage of or manipulated, don't hesitate to intervene as her parent.

Enjoy the opportunity she has to develop lasting personal management skills. If she learns now to discipline herself in these areas, she will be far ahead of the game in later life.

30

Create Photo Albums

WHAT YOU NEED

- advertising fliers
- scissors, colored paper, colorful stickers, small paper cutter (optional)

WHAT TO CHARGE

$8.00 per labeled but undecorated album.
$12.00 to $15.00 per album adorned with colored backgrounds, cropped photos, stickers, etc.

FIND THE CUSTOMER

Circulate your fliers when people seem to be in the mood for organizing—early September when school starts, mid-January after the holidays, late April at spring cleaning time.

Advertise to parents of school-age children. They're taking lots of photos, but most of them don't yet have the time to organize them. Reach those parents through PTA newsletters, ads in school papers, and fliers posted in the library, pediatrician's office, toy store, bookstore, church, health club—any place where they will allow you to advertise.

Ask to make a presentation to women's group meetings, parent support groups, or PTA gatherings. Bring sample albums: one with photos simply organized and arranged and one with decorated pages. Explain briefly what you do and why it would benefit someone to hire you. Distribute fliers with your name and phone number and perhaps an endorsement by a past customer.

START HERE

When someone hires you, make an appointment to meet with her at her earliest convenience. Discuss your fees and your schedule and have the customer show you what photos need organizing. Decide how the project should best be done and inform the customer, if necessary, of the different styles and prices for photo albums. You might even keep a portfolio of that information for your customers' use. Have her choose and purchase photo albums; then return to her home to fill them up with photos.

After you finish the job, insert a small photo of yourself in the back of each album, held down by a sticker that has your name and phone number on it. Every time your customer enjoys her photo album, she'll be reminded, by your smiling face, of who was responsible for making it look so nice.

TRICKS OF THE TRADE

Take a class in photo album design. Check community education programs and gift or party stores for classes. You will learn tasteful, playful, and unique layouts. You will also learn how to incorporate stickers into your page design and how to crop photos for the best visual effect. A class like this will be of great advantage to you.

Take a calligraphy class as well. Your labels will look better and you will be introduced to a whole new world of paper, pens, and other related products.

Work quietly and diligently, avoiding the temptation to comment upon or ask about the customer's photos. Let your employer volunteer information. You concentrate on getting the job done beautifully.

PARENTAL GUIDANCE SUGGESTED

It's satisfying to clean and organize and, at the same time, create something attractive and lasting. Encourage your child to work at both.

Suggest ways that she can streamline her operation, perhaps by developing a filing system that customers use in the initial stage of organization. She can experiment with labels, finding the brand that stick best and look best.

Express enthusiasm any time you see her expending effort in problem-solving or planning. Help her to develop her creative skills by taking her to stores that sell unusual and creative items: stickers, ribbon, albums—anything related to her business.

Brainstorm with her on ideas for displaying and labeling photos and experiment together with page layouts and creative touches.

Always let her own her business; don't impose your advice or help. Instead, with her permission, enjoy the opportunity to put your heads together and have fun.

31

Distribute Coupon Books

Young person with perseverance and creativity needed to design and market a book of coupons. Must sell advertising space to local merchants, creatively arrange each coupon, print and assemble booklets, and distribute throughout neighborhood.

WHAT YOU NEED

☐ phone   ☐ good walking shoes

WHAT TO CHARGE

Ask the advertiser for $30.00 to run his coupon in your book. Have him pay half when he orders the coupon and the other half when the book is distributed. Plan to print and distribute at least 500 books featuring at least 20 local businesses.

FIND THE CUSTOMER

Your first task is to convince the business owners that your coupon book is worth the investment. Your customer needs to be assured that the coupon book will be widely distributed to people who will use it. Decide how many books you will print and when and to whom you will distribute them.

Make an appointment with the business owner and explain clearly and concisely what you want to accomplish. Be prepared to prove to her that you are an honest kid. Show her short letters of reference from a teacher, pastor, or businessperson in the community. Let her know about your personal achievements—a good academic record, leadership positions you have held, community service, etc. Have with you a sample coupon book and written plans that include the date that the book will be printed and specific plans for distribution.

After making your presentation, ask the merchant if you can leave the written proposal with her and come back the following day for her answer. That way she can think about it and even contact references that you provide for her. If she decides to buy space in your book, thank her and ask if she knows of any colleagues that you might contact. Plan to reconnect with your new customer in a few weeks to let her know of your progress and assure her that production is right on schedule.

START HERE

Consider customizing your coupon book or even providing multiple editions, each targeting a specific customer base. For instance, you might want to feature family oriented businesses like restaurants that cater to kids and entertainment options that families would enjoy together. Include coupons for car and appliance repair, pediatricians, bookstores, clothing stores—anything that a family might use. These books you could distribute at school or at church.

In addition, you could design a book for the sports enthusiasts in your town, featuring coupons for health food stores, sports equipment stores, fitness clubs, certified massage therapists, orthopedists, nutritionists, etc. Distribute them at each business represented as well as at a community sports event.

Contact a number of printers for price quotes and advice. Design your coupons, preferably using artwork provided by the customer, so that you can have eight printed on each sheet of paper, checking with your printer well ahead of time to make sure you have set up your designs properly.

Success breeds success in this line of work. Think creatively and present yourself to potential customers, well organized and thoroughly prepared, and business will surely follow. As you prove yourself trustworthy, you will build a solid foundation of repeat customers. Each book will get easier to produce. You will, in addition to making money, gain the admiration and respect of the business community as you build good relationships with your customers, and you will also gain invaluable experience as you participate in thoughtful and fruitful decisions.

TRICKS OF THE TRADE

Your business will be as successful as the impression you make on your customers. Here's how to make a good one:

- Dress neatly and comb your hair.
- Make eye contact when you speak and when you listen.

- Stop by your customer's place of business for a quick hello.
- Be honest always—even when you've made a mistake.

PARENTAL GUIDANCE SUGGESTED

Coupon booklet design and distribution is a lot of work. But as is usually the case, its rewards are comparable to the effort involved. Your child will come into contact with many business people. With your support, she will learn early how to communicate with adults of widely varying personalities.

Help her learn to present herself confidently and intelligently. A young person skilled in making a first impression is skilled indeed. Add to that skill a practiced ease in communicating across the wide range of humanity, and you will have a child leagues ahead of her peers.

Help your child understand the responsibility inherent in an enterprise like this one, but leave the work to her. If she fails to meet her deadlines, she must bear the consequences. It is her responsibility and must always be so. You can, however, help by buying her a time management book or a special calendar to fill out together, underscoring the value of long-range planning and goal setting. Applaud any show of responsibility, always pointing out her successful efforts. Assume that she will follow through as expected and do not give her the impression that you will bail her out if she doesn't. Allow her the learning experience. You'll be glad you did.

32
Help Older People

WHAT YOU NEED

- advertising fliers
- telephone for customers to call
- patience and good manners

WHAT TO CHARGE

$3.00 to $5.00 per hour. Older people are often on fixed incomes and are unable to pay more.

FIND THE CUSTOMER

Ask permission to run an ad in your church bulletin or newsletter. Contact Meals on Wheels or another community agency that provides senior services and ask if they will consider distributing your fliers. Depending on your availability, you may need only one or two clients. Parents and friends can often help by recommending appropriate individuals and by helping you to know what to expect.

START HERE

You can offer to cook, clean, organize, water plants, do laundry, do yard work, or read to your elderly friend. Try to agree ahead of time on a list of chores to be done as well as a time to begin and end your duties for that day.

Perhaps you could, on occasion, bring your client a basket of muffins or other treat. You might call him on days you aren't working, just to check in.

Because your client is so much older than you, he will have a wealth of stories about the past and a lot of interesting information to share. Don't hesitate to ask polite questions. Often your customer will become a very special friend.

TRICKS OF THE TRADE

You can please customers even more with each of these gestures:

- Cut out magazine and newspaper articles on topics that interest them.
- Cut out coupons and sale ads from stores they frequent.
- Pick up inexpensive convenience items they might need: vitamin organizers, a brightly colored case for glasses, a key ring with a miniature flashlight attached.
- Interview them for a school report, letting them know how much you respect their knowledge.

PARENTAL GUIDANCE SUGGESTED

Working for older people can provide enormous benefits to your child. By attentive listening and careful advice, you can facilitate your child's understanding of the challenges, limitations, and advantages of aging, helping him work through possible frustrations in the relationship.

Older people, having grown up through the Depression and war years, often have work ethics and expectations that far exceed the modern child's. You may have to help clarify those expectations and encourage your child to pursue good communication. You might seize the opportunity to train your child in housekeeping skills, finding him more open to learning as he employs those skills elsewhere!

Most important, this opportunity can grow in your child a compassion that is foundational to good character. Patience, kindness, humble service, and maybe even a lifetime friend—anything that develops these qualities is a worthwhile endeavor.

33

Read for the Blind

WHAT YOU NEED

- ☐ advertising fliers
- ☐ telephone for customers to call
- ☐ good reading ability

WHAT TO CHARGE

$3.00 to $5.00 per hour.

FIND THE CUSTOMER

Look in your phone book under the Community Services/Disability Services section, usually found in the front of the book. Call the organizations listed, explaining that you are a kid who loves to read and who reads well. Tell them that you are looking to start a part-time business reading to people with poor or no eyesight and ask how they might refer you.

Post fliers in churches and senior centers (use large print) advertising your service. Talk to church secretaries and administrators of programs for the elderly, explaining your service and asking for referrals.

START HERE

Talk with your potential customer on the phone. Find out what she would like you to read and where and when she needs your service. Make arrangements to meet, making sure you know ahead of time how long you are expected to stay.

Be polite and don't hesitate to ask questions if you are confused.

If things go well, your client will soon become your friend, and you both will look forward to your time together. When you feel comfortable, ask your customer to refer you to others. You might enjoy bringing her an occasional treat, especially on a holiday or special occasion.

TRICKS OF THE TRADE

Don't think that your reading material is limited to newspapers and books. Here are a few fun alternatives:

- Cartoons: Describe the pictures and read the captions.
- Crossword puzzles: Find them in newspapers or puzzle books.
- Plays: Ham it up! Try to get a copy in Braille and act it out together.
- Poetry: You may discover a lasting treasure.
- Your school books: Who knows? Maybe your customer will enjoy your lessons and learn along with you.

PARENTAL GUIDANCE SUGGESTED

Though a problem is unlikely, do not hesitate to monitor the material your child is reading. Do not allow her to read novels or articles that violate your standards. Decide what she should say if presented with material that she's uncomfortable reading. She might simply say, "I need to ask my mom if it's OK to keep reading this. It might be too adult for me. Can I read something else right now?" A calm but honest conversation with your child's customer will probably solve any problems in this area; if not, find a new customer.

Another parental role in this endeavor is to support your child as he builds relationships with each of his clients. Meeting someone for the first time is often uncomfortable. When children are unaccustomed to being around disabled or elderly people, this awkwardness can be compounded. Add the typical trepidations one might feel when performing a service as intimate as reading to a person, and you will see how a child could use the special support and assurance that a parent best provides.

Talk through the child's feelings without a need to correct or admonish him. Be a good listener, and your child will probably work through any difficulties on his own, all the better for it.

Remind the child often that he is performing an important service of compassion. Never, however, diminish the customer by portraying her as someone who needs to be pitied or patronized.

You have a great opportunity to teach your child the value of every individual, that each of us is deserving of dignity and respect, no matter our age or physical condition. In a culture where the elderly and disabled are often thought of as disposable, you have a unique opportunity to help your child see otherwise.

34

Read to Preschoolers

Sensitive, loving reader needed to share good books with young children. Will act as parent helper by regularly engaging children in enjoyable and worthwhile pastime.

WHAT YOU NEED

- advertising fliers and a phone
- reading ability
- library card
- warm heart

WHAT TO CHARGE

$3.00 per half hour.

FIND THE CUSTOMER

Go door to door with your advertising fliers; leave them at bookstores, in the library, and at church. Post them at school. Talk to friends and relatives who have young children. Explain to your potential customers that you're building a business that you enjoy and that benefits both individuals and the community. Tell them you believe that kids can work in ways that are enjoyable, creative, and advantageous to all.

All children need good books in their lives—your customer base is broad and unending. Find statistics on the academic improvement in kids who are regularly read to and share these figures with your potential customers. (One good source among many is Jim Trelease's *The Read Aloud Handbook*.)

Offer to hold story hours at your local bookstore or library. The right book at the right time for the right child can be life-changing, and we know that a steady diet of good books is one of the greatest gifts you can give a child. Preschoolers are enormously receptive to good books; consider extending your service to older children as well.

START HERE

Meet with your customer to decide on a time for your service. Most young children, ages two to five, can stay involved in a story for about a half hour. Some children last much longer. Decide with your customer what length of time would be appropriate for his child.

Offer to provide books from the library unless your customer prefers otherwise. Children love to hear the same story again and again and may want to stick with family favorites. The children's librarian at your school or community library can help you choose the very best books to share with your young listeners. Winners of the Caldecott or Newbery awards are a good place to start, and there are hundreds of other excellent books available.

When reading aloud, be sure to keep frequent eye contact with the children, occasionally stopping the narrative to ask a child what might happen next or to point out a funny or interesting picture. You can involve a wiggly listener by having him turn pages for you, repeat key phrases, or even act out parts of the story. Keep your voice animated, varying speed and pitch as the story warrants. You may want to attend a story time at the library and watch the reader's technique.

TRICKS OF THE TRADE

- Personalize your book selections to the listener's interest and age and to the appropriate season.
- Bring a prop to match the story—a bowl of porridge, mittens, chocolate chip cookies!
- Teach kids a poem to recite, a song to sing, a story to act out, and then perform for parents.

PARENTAL GUIDANCE SUGGESTED

This job truly provides a service to the community and will benefit your child in a number of ways. Her reading skills, no matter how good, will improve, as will her interpersonal skills. Her research and library skills will broaden, and she will benefit, regardless of her age, from exposure to the many artistic and literary virtuosos publishing books for children.

Support her by driving her frequently to the library and to bookstores, by helping her gather helpful information, and by discussing enthusiastically the various aspects of her job. Consider subscribing to a children's book review service. Take her to author signings and other literary events. Encourage her to use her growing skills widely and creatively, reminding her frequently of the impact she is having on her listeners and on the community at large.

35

Read for Hospitals

Gregarious, self-directed young person needed to recruit and organize peers to read to hospitalized kids. Funding not available from hospitals. Must be willing to approach community service groups for financial support.

WHAT YOU NEED

☐ motivation and organizational skills

☐ access to great books

WHAT TO CHARGE

$5.00 to $7.00 per hour.

FIND THE CUSTOMER

You have to go at this exciting venture in two directions, because essentially you have two sets of customers —those who support your service financially and those who receive your service. First, recruit a small but impressive team of students who are willing to spend between one and three hours a week reading to kids who are hospitalized.

Second, write a short proposal outlining your plan. Explain in a paragraph or two how you think your idea will benefit sick and frightened children as well as the young people who will entertain and distract them by sharing good stories. Some may think that reading to hospitalized children should be strictly a charitable activity. You need to help them see the other aspect of your venture—creating job opportunities for young people that enable them to serve the community, building positive links to both individuals and organizations. Briefly introduce the members of your reading team, profiling some of their personal achievements and positive characteristics. Type up your proposal (make sure it's free of mistakes!) and put it in a fancy folder.

Third, approach the hospital administrator with your idea, asking for permission to continue your pursuit.

Fourth, present your plan to your church elder board, your youth group, or community service organizations such as Rotary Club, Kiwanis, Elks, or Junior Women's League. Ask one or more groups to support your venture financially so that you can pay your readers an hourly wage, thereby employing young people in a character-building occupation for the good of the community.

When you obtain funding, your responsibilities will shift to scheduling and overseeing your peers, communicating with hospital personnel, and managing payment. Pay your readers for their time spent with the children. Pay yourself for the time you spend administrating the program. Keep careful, clean records of your time.

START HERE

Each step you take along the way is crucial to your future success. You will establish credibility if your idea is well articulated and your plan well presented. Though this type of business is not traditional, especially among young people, it affords tremendous opportunity for good and is worth whatever effort involved to convince potential donors of its value.

You will have to keep detailed transactions of money coming in and money going out. It would be wise to arrange to be supervised by an officer of whatever organization is funding your project. After winning approval of your venture by the hospital staff, you may want to arrange a meeting with a pediatric nurse who can help you and your staff understand how best to work with the children and how best to cooperate with the nursing staff.

Your communication skills and organizational abilities will grow, probably quite significantly, but it is your character that will be most deeply affected by serving both peers and families in your community.

TRICKS OF THE TRADE

- Ask for and listen to advice.
- Dress neatly and look clean and sharp when you're on the job.
- Respect the demands made on the time and energy of working health care professionals.
- Be patient but persuasive.

PARENTAL GUIDANCE SUGGESTED

Your guidance and wise counsel in a venture of this kind will be your child's very best resource. Entering into the world of adults in this way, even to accomplish good, can be intimidating and confusing. You are a crucial ally. Help your child to set up a system whereby he is protected through accountability. Supervise his record keeping and scheduling so that you can back him up if donor organizations or youth employees ever question him.

Help him communicate professionally with the many adults with whom he will be interacting. Be generous but judicial with advice; be your child's greatest fan as he moves to set up an organization with these multiple purposes. He will learn much through the process and hopefully build an organization that raises the esteem of young people throughout the entire community and beyond.

36

Organize Toys

WHAT YOU NEED

☐ advertising fliers ☐ a creative eye

Let customers supply necessary storage bins or boxes according to your recommendations.

WHAT TO CHARGE

$4.00 to $6.00 per hour.

FIND THE CUSTOMER

Ask the coordinator of women's ministries at your church if you can present your service at a meeting of young mothers. Leave fliers at a moms' support group function. Go door to door in your neighborhood with a small box full of Legos, broken doll parts, marbles, pieces of a Happy Meal box, sticky candy, game pieces—all the things that can collect in a kid's room.

Give the potential customer a good look at the mess, then show her another box, clean and organized, with a place for everything. (Small, inexpensive organizers can be found at any drugstore or grocery store in the housewares department.) Tell her that you are a responsible kid who would be glad to similarly transform her child's room.

Let her know that you will shop for organizers—plastic bins, stackable boxes, shelving, etc.—as she requests, and arrange the child's possessions neatly inside. Tell her that with all the things she has to do, you suspect that it's hard to find time for such a task. You are here to help!

START HERE

Ask which toys are most often played with and what usually causes the mess. Determine with your customer what kind of additional storage, if any, would help the problem. Have a detailed description of the various plastic bins and buckets available in area stores and offer to shop for your customer's choice of items. Present her with a price list and figure the cost. Your customer can pay ahead of time or you can use your own money and get reimbursed upon delivery. You may be able to speak with the store manager and obtain a discount, which you can happily pass along to your customer.

You might ask permission to take discarded toys to a missions organization or homeless shelter, thereby accomplishing two good things.

Your service can extend to closets and clothing, bathrooms—even garages, if you're very brave and energetic.

Make sure that you are well informed about the various storage options available and that you consider your suggestions carefully. If your customer opts not to buy storage items, work to carefully organize the existing space, thinking hard about what will work best.

TRICKS OF THE TRADE

- Take time with your customers. Don't rush their decisions even if they take longer than you would like.
- Make suggestions using phrases such as "Maybe you would like . . ." and "Would you consider . . ." so that they can listen to your thoughts without feeling like they're being railroaded.
- Never stop to play with a toy that interests you. Tempting as it may be to explore your customers' stuff, it's mighty unprofessional.

PARENTAL GUIDANCE SUGGESTED

If yours is the rare child who is by nature orderly, consider yourself among the blessed and encourage him to do what comes naturally. Creating order from chaos is not just satisfying; it's a highly valued life skill.

If he doesn't drive, perhaps you can set aside one or two days each week to take him to the store to shop for supplies. Help him make wise decisions by acting as a sounding board. Gather information for him and with him, watching for sales, passing along pertinent articles and books, actively problem-solving with him. Enjoy your role as a consultant, helping him see the big picture but letting him make his own careful decisions. He will appreciate being treated as an expert in his field, and you will enjoy a new dynamic in your relationship with him.

37

Publish a Magazine

Creative, motivated young person needed to write, copy, and circulate a magazine for neighborhood children, Sunday school classes, or youth groups. Must love to share helpful, funny, inspirational information geared to young children or peers.

WHAT YOU NEED

- [ ] typewriter or computer word processor
- [ ] access to copy machine
- [ ] stapler
- [ ] reference material
- [ ] notebook for subscriber information

WHAT TO CHARGE

For a semimonthly publication (two issues each month), charge $3.00 per month. If you sell 15 subscriptions, you'll make $45.00 a month minus your copying costs. To make more money, publish more often or sell more subscriptions.

FIND THE CUSTOMER

Produce a sample issue and make several copies. Distribute your copies among your potential customers, asking if they might be interested in a subscription to your fine publication. Include in that first issue a publication schedule and a short list of ideas for future issues.

Let your customer know that while this is a money-making venture for you it is also an opportunity for you to serve your community with your knowledge and skill in this area. Assure your customer that each issue will arrive on time (be sure that it does!) and will be of high quality and in excellent taste.

When your customer enthusiastically agrees to subscribe, write him a receipt and add his name and pertinent information to your subscription notebook.

START HERE

Decide who you want to target (neighborhood kids, church kids, classmates, etc.) and what you want to communicate (Bible study ideas, book reviews, neighborhood news, creative writing, recipes, money-making ideas!).

Decide how long your newsletter should be and in what format (folded in half, folded in thirds, flat with staples in one corner, arranged like a newspaper, etc.)

You may want to bring in a partner to help you and split the responsibilities and profits. If so, carefully write out job descriptions for each person involved so that the work load is divided fairly and you both know what to expect of each other. Plan to meet regularly to see if your system is working fairly and properly. Partners must always communicate. If they don't, disaster is likely to strike.

When you have dealt with the who, what, why, how much, and how often, you are ready to start gathering or producing your material. If you have access to and knowledge of a word processor, you will have an easier time typing and perfecting your articles. Enjoy the chance to communicate what interests you and what you think will interest your subscribers. Always be sure that your material is of the highest quality, honoring God and others.

If you stick to your publication schedule and exhibit creativity and high standards, your circulation will increase rapidly, and so will your bank balance. Most important, you will be in a position to influence many young minds, thereby making a substantial and long-lasting difference in the world.

TRICKS OF THE TRADE

- Continually improve your material. You can't afford to bore your customer: Always look for clearer, more interesting ways to display your material.
- Know your audience. Find out what your readers want. Try to satisfy and surprise them.

PARENTAL GUIDANCE SUGGESTED

This enterprise is full of opportunity. Your child can build formidable skills in analysis, planning, writing, designing, organizing—the list seems endless. Your support is crucial. Help her think through the seemingly mountainous amount of detail, strategizing with her for efficiency and quality in her publishing business.

Check out biographies from the library and read to her about journalists, writers of fiction and poetry, and publishers and publications that have changed the course of history. Help her understand that all writers were once children and that some may have started just as she has.

Review her written or chosen material to make sure it

meets standards of honor and graciousness. Study what the Bible says about how we should communicate to others. Teach her especially the different kinds of humor so that she will understand what is God-honoring and what is not.

Help her establish a form and a structure for her publication so that she will experience the freedom of following her own rules. Then help her explore her creativity within the limits of the rules.

Take her to visit newspaper and magazine publishers, helping her learn the business from many perspectives.

The possibilities for learning in this business are endless and exciting. Enjoy it!

38

Photograph People

WHAT YOU NEED

- advertising fliers
- good camera
- calendar

WHAT TO CHARGE

$7.00 to $10.00 per hour, plus the cost of film and developing.

FIND THE CUSTOMER

Distribute fliers throughout your neighborhood. Ask permission to display your fliers at party supply stores, florists, balloon shops, and gift stores. Send fliers and a cover letter to professional party planners and disc jockeys asking for referrals and promising the same. Talk to the wedding coordinators at churches in your area.

Explain in person and in your flier that you are not a professional photographer but a talented amateur who is considerably less costly and can simply record the event and its attendees, leaving the formal portraits to the expensive professional.

START HERE

Ask to meet with your customer a week before the party. Arrive, notebook in hand, to write down specifically who and what the host wants you to photograph and how many rolls of film he wants you to shoot. On the day of the party, come half an hour early, neatly dressed and fully supplied, bringing extra fliers in case a party guest asks about your service.

Try to take a picture of each party-goer, being always polite and unobtrusive. Pay close attention to the events of the day so that you don't miss any cake-cutting, bouquet-throwing, or other important rituals.

After the party, check in with the host, letting him know how many rolls of film you have ready to be developed and when the finished pictures will be delivered.

When you deliver your pictures, be sure to attach several fliers to the envelopes. If your customer is pleased with what he has received, ask him for a referral. Success in this job will come not only from consistently high quality photos but also from the manner in which you communicate with your customers and their guests. Your mature and polite demeanor will impress the adults around you and insure their interest in trying out your service for their next celebration.

TRICKS OF THE TRADE

Learn to focus and shoot quickly. Your candid shots will be much better if people are generally unaware of your presence. Take a variety of shots including some close-ups, especially of children. Special memories are enhanced by intimate close-ups of family members and friends.

If you're looking for something to shoot, offer to take some casual, portrait-style pictures of couples and families. Your host or hostess will appreciate having them and may even be able to use them for gifts.

PARENTAL GUIDANCE SUGGESTED

There are a number of ways in which you can support your child in this business, most of which are very basic. Help him dress appropriately for each occasion. Help him know how best to address the party guests and present himself to his customers.

You might encourage him to take a photography class at a local community college. If there is none available, he can ask for a few short lessons from a professional and check out books from the library. You can also discuss with him what photos in your family collection are especially memorable and why.

You can teach him how to make a small child respond and how best to photograph shy people. You can treat him like a budding professional and let him gain plenty of experience taking pictures of your family events. Your enthusiastic approval of what he is doing and your genuine support of his independence will powerfully enable him to succeed both personally and professionally.

39

Perform Puppet Shows

Enterprising young puppeteer with a flair for theatrics needed to entertain young children at parties, church classes, and school events. Will produce and perform a puppet show appropriate to the occasion.

WHAT YOU NEED

- ☐ advertising fliers and a phone
- ☐ a variety of scripts
- ☐ a puppet stage
- ☐ puppets
- ☐ an assistant or two (optional)

WHAT TO CHARGE

$25.00 per presentation.

FIND THE CUSTOMER

Go door to door with your puppets, letting them make the sales pitch for you. At each house leave a flier that includes a quote or two from a happy customer. Ask for permission to set up your puppet theater outside a party supply store or outside your grocery store. Circulate your flier at your school and church. Let people know that your high-quality show is put on by kids and for kids.

START HERE

The most important part of your show is your script. Ask the librarian to direct you to books of scripts specifically for puppet theater. *Fantastic Theater* by Judy Sierra has everything you need to know about puppets and puppet theater, featuring thirty scripted plays from around the world.

Most children's book review publications (*The Horn Book, School Library Journal, The Bulletin of the Center for Children's Books*) have advertisements listing companies that specialize in scripts. One such company is PLAYS, Inc., 120 Boylston Street, Boston, MA 02116-4615. They can send you short, entertaining scripts just for kids, even some with holiday themes.

After choosing your script, you need to buy or make your puppets and your puppet theater. Again you will find that your library is a great source of information. Hundreds of styles of puppets and theaters can be bought or made. You will enjoy deciding what type best communicates your script.

Oftentimes, the most effective puppets are homemade. They needn't be fancy or expensive. It is the most powerful tool of your mind—imagination—that will make the puppet come alive. Plan to spend a significant amount of time perfecting your show. Mediocre puppet shows are easy to find. You want the word to spread that your show is worth booking.

If you know an adult who is involved in theater, consider asking advice. You will enjoy more business and enjoy your business more if your show is something to be proud of. When your show is ready, go out and sell it. Always be on time to your engagements and always treat your customer with respect. Never forget that shows are worthless without an audience and that you are there to serve, not to be served.

After each performance write your customer a note of thanks and include a flier or your business card. Tell her you appreciate any referrals. Puppet theater can provide you with excellent experience in performance and in public relations. And if well done, it can give you the deep satisfaction of delighting, instructing, and entertaining the precious minds of young children.

TRICKS OF THE TRADE

Judge the quality of any show for children by how much you yourself enjoy it. If you think it's dumb, so will younger children. If you think it's great and it keeps your attention, expect it to do the same for your audience.

Beware of using violence, silly as it may be. Laughter can be generated by means other than your characters hitting, pulling hair, dismembering each other, and so on. Your show will have more integrity, your audience will be less distracted, and parents will trust you more if you use other means of humor.

The more kids interact with your characters and props, the more they will enjoy your show. Have them repeat phrases, yell warnings, and make sound effects.

PARENTAL GUIDANCE SUGGESTED

Kids with a natural interest in theater will enjoy this business. They may, however, need extra encouragement in the less glamorous aspects of dramatic production such as record-keeping and other organizational tasks. Help your child understand that diligence in those areas is as important as good performance and that the most successful dramatists are only so because they have been properly managed.

Young actors also need to be encouraged to rehearse, rehearse, rehearse. Few kids understand that powerful presentations are the result of hours of meticulous attention to detail. Be willing to serve as critic, making suggestions very carefully.

Try to attend the rehearsal of a professional stage production, letting your child see firsthand the hard working atmosphere of theater. Help your youngster see that every actor or actress must be teachable to be good. Recognizing the value of good preparation will serve your child well, as will the resulting experiences of success.

Puppet theater can be fun and exciting for the whole family. Enjoy the growth in your child as she faces the highs and lows of live performance while learning to communicate responsibly to children and adults alike.

40

Form a Science Club

WHAT YOU NEED

- ☐ advertising fliers and a phone
- ☐ a source for good ideas
- ☐ appropriate materials
- ☐ a location

WHAT TO CHARGE

If your science club meets once a month, charge $10.00 per kid, per month. You would be wise to limit your students to about 15. Even if you spend $50.00 each month for materials, you're still making $100.00 a month! If you run two or three clubs, repeating lessons, you can make a lot of money improving the science skills of kids in your community.

FIND THE CUSTOMER

Circulate fliers throughout the neighborhood, at church, and at school. Contact home-school support groups and arrange to make a presentation at a monthly meeting. Talk to the owners of nature and toy stores in your area, asking to post fliers in their stores. On your flier, list exactly what your classes will be studying.

You should target a specific age group, first through third graders in one group, fourth through sixth graders in another. List the time, date, and location for your club and a phone number to call to register.

START HERE

Go to the local elementary school, explain your plan, and ask to borrow a textbook or two appropriate to the age group you'll be targeting. Plan to center your program loosely around the areas of study outlined in the book but expand beyond what the kids learn in school.

Or if you have a particular area of interest, electronics or biology for instance, feel free to design your club around that field of study. Be limited only by what is safe and interesting to kids. Plan to spend about an hour for each lesson and experiment.

Check your local bookstore or nature store for the many outstanding science books available. *Backyard Scientist*, the *Eyewitness* books, and the *Usborne* series are all full of experiments for kids to do at home or at your science club.

Well planned and carried out, your science club could prove to be extremely popular, complete with long waiting lists. You will have reason to be proud of a business that provides steady income as well as a great service to the community.

TRICKS OF THE TRADE

Plan a program that would keep your attention. In other words, don't "dumb it down" for younger kids. They will enjoy a challenge much more than they will condescending material.

Ask an adult to attend your class to help with any behavioral challenges.

It is important that kids get as much hands-on experience as possible. Though you won't cover material as quickly as you would if the kids simply read the textbook, they will retain the information longer and understand the concepts much better if they see and touch for themselves.

PARENTAL GUIDANCE SUGGESTED

This outlet for science enthusiasts serves multiple purposes. Your child will learn crucial planning and organizational skills as he engages younger children in experimentation and discussion. He will significantly reinforce his own knowledge as he passes it on to his students. He will also gain recognition in the community for his creative service.

He will need you to supervise his program for safety and age appropriateness. And he will need your quiet support at each meeting to assure order as well as your continued encouragement as he works the bugs out of his presentation.

A tremendous opportunity for the development of leadership skills, a science club will benefit your child in a myriad of ways while serving the needs of your community.

41

Tutor Young
Athletes

> Talented athlete needed to share skills
> and experience with younger kids. Must
> be patient, encouraging, and willing to
> teach basics.

WHAT YOU NEED

□ advertising fliers

□ basic sports equipment:
bats, balls, mitts, etc.

WHAT TO CHARGE

$5.00 per half hour.

FIND THE CUSTOMER

Contact a support group for single mothers and ask to
make a presentation at their next meeting. Single moms
often do not have time for games of catch or batting practice, but they want their children to enjoy and develop
competency in these skills. You may find that they especially appreciate your offer of service. Other advertising
ideas:

- Ask permission to distribute your fliers at your school's PTA meeting.
- Contact your city's Little League and soccer commissioners and ask to make a short presentation and leave fliers at the next coaches' meeting.
- Ask the manager of the sporting goods store if you can leave your flier on the counter.
- Advertise in the newspaper.
- Post fliers at your church and school.
- Wear T-shirts with your company name printed in bold, bright letters.
- Spread the word about your unique service at summer camps, after school programs, YMCA programs—anywhere there are kids!

START HERE

As a sports tutor, you will work with the child's mind as much as with her movement. Build her confidence any way you can; doing so will be the single most effective way to improve her skills. Point out every good thing she does, even if you have to work hard to find it. Give her ample time to practice, letting her know that our bodies learn by repetition and it's both necessary and good to do things over and over as we patiently edge toward improvement.

If you provide large amounts of encouragement, relaxed and enjoyable practice, and just a little direct instruction, your young customer will look forward to her lessons and will most likely improve her skills considerably. As a consequence, her parent will retain your services and let others know what an excellent job you're doing. Your business will flourish.

TRICKS OF THE TRADE

Decide which skills you are qualified to handle, listing them in your promotional material. It's better to do a great job in one or two sports than a mediocre job in many sports.

What kids usually need is a patient friend to spend time practicing simple skills, as opposed to a world class kinesiologist.

Try to make exercises as varied as possible while reinforcing the same skill.

PARENTAL GUIDANCE SUGGESTED

If your child feels qualified to be a sports tutor, chances are her skills in athletics are well established. It is not, however, athletic prowess that will make her successful in this endeavor. It is her relational skills that will be called upon the most. You can encourage her to make specific lesson plans for each young customer using creative games and skill builders that are fun. You can help her learn to concentrate on the positive (hopefully by example).

You can teach her to teach, helping her communicate in many different ways to accommodate the different means by which children learn. Go with her to observe different coaches in action. Critically evaluate their effectiveness, comparing one style to another. Find books and articles on master teachers and discover why they excel in their profession. Read material on child development, establishing a reasonable set of expectations for children of varying ages.

Remember, this is not a job for a job's sake. It is a marvelous learning experience for your child.

42

Tend Children

Patient, energetic, creative person who enjoys the company of young children needed to serve as nanny to a busy family. Must be extraordinarily conscientious and willing to initiate interesting activity.

WHAT TO CHARGE

$3.00 per hour.

FIND THE CUSTOMER

Young mothers are always on the lookout for baby-sitters who are worthy of their children. That means someone who is near perfect—warm and loving, absolutely responsible, dependable, respectable, resourceful, and fun to have around. If you fit the bill, chances are your customer will find you.

If you're just starting out, you may have to let the world know who you are and just how capable you are. Though you can circulate fliers to advertise your services, it seems more prudent to find your employer by word of mouth.

After all, you may not want to be hired by just any family. Spending a summer in a house full of uncontrollable children is nightmarish at best.

Your parents and older friends may be your best resource for finding a family with already well-disciplined and well-cared-for kids. Discuss with them your plans and ask for their help in finding you the right opportunity. Chances are they will, and that mother with the high standards will, to her good fortune, find you.

START HERE

Baby-sitting can be a tedious and annoying job or it can be fulfilling and joyful—it's up to you. Call upon your initiative and intelligence, and you will find yourself receiving far more than you give. By planning activities that educate and entertain, you and your children will laugh and learn together, keeping everyone, especially your employers, happy.

Find some books on activities appropriate for children. There are multitudes in the library. Talk to friends who you think make excellent baby-sitters and to mothers whose children you know are happy and well-adjusted. Ask them for advice and ideas as to how you can do your job justice or just spend time observing their interaction with children. You can learn a lot that way.

As with any job, whatever you put into it comes back better. You will be employed to care for the singularly most important thing on earth—a child. Give it all you've got.

TRICKS OF THE TRADE

To prepare for such a task, first take a baby-sitting class at your Red Cross office or YMCA. You will learn crucial first aid skills, basic child development, and baby care.

You will also have a chance to discuss what qualities make a superior sitter.

Put together a list of emergency phone numbers. In most area codes, you can reach any medical personnel or sheriff by dialing 911. Make sure you have the number for poison control and the emergency room. It's not a bad idea to write down your home phone number and the address and phone number of the home where you are sitting to give to emergency personnel.

Look around for something you can do to impress and please your employer. Fold the clothes, do the dishes, sweep the floor. Doing these chores could be the best public relations move you've ever made.

PARENTAL GUIDANCE SUGGESTED

Though the common response to the suggestion of baby-sitting as a profession is a yawn, you can teach your child the value of purposeful and focused child care. Discuss frequently and seriously the many skills required in such a job, helping your child internalize the understanding that hers is a profession fraught with importance.

Take this often ignored opportunity to teach her that children are of such enormous value that only the best of the best is good enough. In doing so you will communicate not only the truth but love for her by implication. Help her work through the countless difficulties inherent in caring for children, pointing out areas where she has found success through understanding and resourcefulness.

Support her efforts to provide activities for the children, making suggestions and guiding her toward resources you know will be helpful. Above all, treat her job with sincere respect, acknowledging its challenges and sharing its joys.

43

Tutor Children

> Capable communicator who excels in academics needed to tutor other kids. Must be patient and understanding.

WHAT YOU NEED

- advertising fliers
- alternative resource material

WHAT TO CHARGE

$3.00 to $5.00 per hour.

FIND THE CUSTOMER

Circulate your fliers around the neighborhood. Run an ad in the newsletter of any elementary school in your area. If the PTA has a newsletter, ask to advertise there too. Don't forget about private and alternative schools. Give teachers a supply of your fliers to pass on to parents of students who may be struggling. Post your flier on the church bulletin board.

START HERE

Find a book in the library about learning styles. Often the reason certain students struggle in school is because they do not absorb material in the way it is being taught. In math, for instance, some students need to touch real objects to understand corresponding concepts. They need to stack blocks in groups to fully internalize multiplication and cut objects apart to fully grasp fractions.

In reading, some students remember much better what they have heard, some what they have seen. It could be that the student you are tutoring is bright and capable but needs the material presented in a way more in tune with his learning style. Take time to educate yourself about these and perhaps other issues in the art of teaching. You may enable the student to make enormous breakthroughs because of your knowledge about how people learn.

On the other hand, some students are unmotivated because they feel like failures already. Some have little interest in academic work but are under the thumb of a parent or teacher. A few, only a very few, have reduced capabilities. Tutoring can be challenging as you attempt to unlock the mysteries of your student's troubles.

You must be patient, doing your best to teach through encouragement and positive reinforcement. Take an interest in your student's private life. Besides gaining insight into some of his roadblocks to learning, you will be better able to provide encouragement if your student recognizes in you genuine caring and friendship. In fact, it may be your friendship more than your tutoring that helps your student the most.

TRICKS OF THE TRADE

Don't forget that you are employed by your student's parents. Cultivate good communication, showing them by your promptness, respectful conversation, and focused attention that you are indeed a worthy employee.

Try some unorthodox teaching methods that will surprise your student. Post math facts on the ceiling above her bed. Give her bread to nibble into the shape of continents. Learn fractions by making cookies and doubling or fifteen sixteenthing the recipe. Create memorable learning experiences.

PARENTAL GUIDANCE SUGGESTED

Tutoring can be frustrating for good learners who can't imagine how their student cannot get what seems so obvious. You can help facilitate patience and compassion by helping your child understand some of the components of learning.

Often, a student fails simply because he is overwhelmed by the emotional pain of an abusive or broken family or other similar tragic circumstance in his life. Sensitize your more fortunate child to factors such as these and brainstorm some creative ways to make learning easier for kids who struggle.

Be a partner when it comes to problem solving. There will be plenty of it in the beginning but undoubtedly, as your child begins to understand the nature of learning and the art of teaching, you will see him develop some wings of his own and an understanding born of experience.

44

Sell Snacks

Gregarious young chef needed to make delectable snacks and drinks to sell to people who are hungry and thirsty.

WHAT YOU NEED

- a safe but busy place to sell your wares
- a display table, cart, or booth
- a few big signs
- equipment and supplies for whatever you choose to make
- appropriate storage containers to keep food hot, cold, and fresh
- a safe place for your money
- napkins, plastic utensils —whatever your snack of choice requires

WHAT TO CHARGE

Figure the cost of your product and double it. Don't forget to add in expenses for things like Styrofoam cups, if you're making hot chocolate, or Popsicle sticks and wax paper, if you're making caramel apples.

Try to purchase in large quantities; you'll save a lot

more in the long run. All in all, try to keep your selling prices between $.50 and $1.50 per item.

FIND THE CUSTOMER

Customers will be attracted by your brightly decorated table or stand. Try to sell your products from something that is both portable and attractive. You can go so far as to make a sign that attaches to a tall structure of PVC pipe or wood. Or, you might just use a bike flag pole and tie bright shiny ribbons that flutter in the breeze and catch people's eyes.

Make a list of your items using words that will make people want to buy. Advertise "Thick, creamy hot chocolate," "Warm, freshly-baked cinnamon buns," "Icy cold orange juice," "Healthy, sugar-free juice bars."

While this job leaves you much freedom to work where and when you want, you would be wise to make regular appearances. You might sell at a certain office complex every Monday afternoon or at the park every Saturday morning. People will begin to expect you, to look forward to your treats. You will develop regulars who will surely spread the word among their friends. Your business will grow.

START HERE

Offer unique food items. A bunch of bananas will probably not generate a lot of excitement in your clientele, but dip those bananas in chocolate, roll them in crushed cashew nuts, freeze them, and—well, that's another thing.

Offer healthy items. Though it's tempting to make only delectable desserts, many of your customers are health and weight conscious. Bran muffins, homemade trail mix, fruit pops, fresh juices—foods such as these will appeal to a broader spectrum of buyers. If you're selling at a park or baseball field, you're likely to sell a lot more snacks to children if you offer treats that are yummy and healthy at the same time.

Offer only a few specialties. You are not in the restaurant business, so don't feel that you have to appeal to the full range of tastes and appetites. Make no more than three different foods, but make them well.

Have a knowledgeable adult advise you on proper handling and storage of food. You don't want to find out that customers got sick after eating your bagels and cream cheese, which had been sitting in the hot sun for hours. Make sure your snacks won't spoil and that the methods you use to prepare them are safe and healthy.

TRICKS OF THE TRADE

Be charming. Just the fact that you're a kid will bring you some business, but when people discover that you're a bright, smiling, talkative kid who greets his customers warmly and even remembers his regulars' names, your business will boom.

Tailor your snacks to the season. Offer candied apples and hot cider in the fall, fruit pops or chocolate-dipped strawberries in the summer, hot chocolate in winter—people love to celebrate the season with special foods.

Take care to package your snacks attractively. A bit of red ribbon, a candy pumpkin, even a brightly colored stirring spoon—these extras lend uniqueness to your business. People will love your creativity and buy accordingly.

Carefully keep track of your sales and expenses so that you can evaluate your progress. Make a chart to determine which items are selling the best and which bring in the most money. Make your future decisions according to what your records and charts tell you.

It is unlikely that you will need a permit from the county health department to sell your snacks, but call to make sure. Someone there can advise you about how to handle your food items to ensure the safety and health of your customers.

PARENTAL GUIDANCE SUGGESTED

You function as the safety monitor on all fronts. Make sure your child's food items are safely prepared and stored. Make sure he is selling in a secure and well supervised location. Be willing to accompany him until you are convinced he will be safe.

Make sure that his money is protected, and that he is completely comfortable with handling money and making change. Practice with him. Make sure he can communicate well with adults and that he can protect himself from someone who makes him feel uncomfortable.

Have fun along with your child, experimenting with recipes, making signs, and planning. Always give him full responsibility for the success of his business; enjoy your role as a consultant only. Whether his snack stand grows into an international franchise or just services the four kids who live on your block, the experience of it will do him a world of good. He will learn and so will you. Enjoy the process.

45

Pull Weeds

WHAT YOU NEED

- advertising fliers
- a well-fitting, sturdy pair of gloves
- plastic trash bags with twist ties
- a water bottle
- portable tape player or radio with earphones (optional)

WHAT TO CHARGE

$3.50 to $5.00 per hour.

FIND THE CUSTOMER

Circulate your fliers throughout the neighborhood. Then go door to door, introducing yourself and telling people that you can save them time and trouble by doing their weeding for them. If you have weeded at a house nearby or, better yet, at your own house, invite the potential customers to walk over and inspect the quality of your work.

START HERE

The best time to pull weeds is in early spring when the ground is wet from frequent rain and the weeds have just begun to flourish. Pull from the very bottom of the weed so that you can bring up the entire root system. Make it a game to see how many plants you can get, roots and all. Put all the weeds in a single pile, then periodically load the pile into a plastic garbage bag that you bring with you. You may want to save some of the weeds to carry with you when you make sales calls. Let potential customers see how many you can pull in one hour.

Try to do as thorough a job as you can. Make sure the customer can see a dramatic difference by the time you're through.

If you listen to a radio or tape player, always keep the volume down so you can hear if the customer calls for you.

TRICKS OF THE TRADE

Make a large stand-up sign to put out in front of the house where you're working. It can read "Danny Blaise, age 8, is pulling weeds here. If you have weeds to pull, call 555-9876." People walking or driving by will read the sign and call you. You might even build a flier holder into your sign so that they have access to your fliers as well.

Bring a broom to sweep the driveway or walkway or whatever surface you may inadvertently fling dirt upon. Even if most of the dirt didn't come from your weed pulling, sweep it anyway. Your customer will love it.

Wear a watch so you know exactly how much time has passed. If you stop for a long rest or a conversation with someone, deduct the time from your hours. Bring a paper and pencil, if necessary, to help figure it out correctly.

Always remember to thank your employer, even if you're exhausted and can't wait to leave. Be grateful for having been hired and always be polite enough to say thank you.

PARENTAL GUIDANCE SUGGESTED

Weed pulling opportunities are nearly as ubiquitous as weeds themselves. A host of grown-up ills—bad backs, bad knees, bad schedules—work in your child's favor as she looks for willing customers.

Your role will probably be to keep her motivated. Starting a new job is exciting. Staying with it is a challenge. Help her determine realistic expectations. It's better to work a half hour on a weekday afternoon and make $1.25 than it is to work seven hours on a hot Saturday, make a bundle, and never want to work again.

Let her own her success. If she does a great job, avoid saying "I'm so proud of you." Instead, say, "I'll bet you feel great about the job you did. I sure would if I were you." Though it seems like a subtle difference, by so phrasing your approval, you help her take responsibility for what she has done. You teach her the importance of taking pride in work because it feels good and right, not because it gains the approval of others. Perhaps if more children were taught to value their own efforts, we could avoid part of the current crisis in business ethics.

46

Rake Leaves

Energetic and self-motivated youngster to rake and bag leaves during the fall season for customers who don't have the time or physical capacity to do it themselves.

WHAT YOU NEED

- advertising fliers
- a sturdy but lightweight rake
- a pair of gloves
- a lightweight trash can
- large plastic garbage bags

WHAT TO CHARGE

$4.00 to $6.00 per hour.

FIND THE CUSTOMER

Go door to door with your fliers early in the fall. Bring your rake and a bag of leaves with you. Tell your customers that you will save them time and an aching back by raking and bagging their leaves for them.

If you have raked at a house nearby, invite your potential customer to look at the great job you did at the neighbor's house. Tell him you'd be glad to make his yard look just as nice.

If you live in a neighborhood where there are enormous amounts of leaves to be raked, consider starting a "raking brigade." Gather three friends to work as a team. Charge a flat fee depending on the size of the yard and cover three times as many yards in a day. Pay yourself a little more than your companions for your role as administrator, and make sure that work gets done quickly and done well. Advertise heavily ahead of time so the whole neighborhood knows that on a certain Saturday, the leaf brigade is coming! If you really want to be enterprising, organize a block party at the same time. That way you'll get all the neighbors involved (who could resist?), draw a lot of attention to your business, and provide fun for the whole neighborhood.

START HERE

Write down your appointments in a notebook as you make them. Set aside one day to sell your service and another day to provide it. You can keep your time better organized that way, plus you'll be able to dress up to meet your neighbors, saving your scrappy work clothes for the job.

Here's the best method for handling great quantities of leaves. Rake the leaves into a pile. Pick up armfuls with the rake and one arm. Dump the leaves into a trash can lined with a plastic bag. When the bag is full, pull it out and put a twist tie on it. The trash can is essential because it holds the bag open for you.

TRICKS OF THE TRADE

Make a big free-standing sign to put out in front of the house where you're working. It can read "Dustin Skylar, age 10, is raking leaves here. If you want your leaves raked, call 555-4567." Construct your sign so that it will hold your fliers. If anyone is walking or driving by, they can pick one up.

When your neighbor's lawn begins to fill up with leaves again, take yourself and your big smile back over and offer to rake again. Remember that if you've done a great job the first time, you'll very likely get that second chance.

PARENTAL GUIDANCE SUGGESTED

The nice thing about raking leaves is that you can see the results of your labor. Point out to your child often how nice the yards that he has raked look. Say things like "You must feel great when you see these clean yards. I know Mr. and Mrs. Bennett sure appreciate what you did." Or "I'll bet it's satisfying to know you've helped out the Harris family." Let your child know that you acknowledge and take pride in his good work, but that the person who should feel the best is him.

Raking leaves is hard physical labor, especially for little people. Allow your child to express feelings of discouragement or frustration. Let him know that it is perfectly normal to feel such things. After you have patiently and seriously heard him out, say "I wonder what other leaf-rakers do to make things a little easier." Hopefully your child will come up with his own solutions for making his job better. Allow him the chance to do so, thereby demonstrating your confidence in his capabilities.

47

Operate an Info Line

WHAT YOU NEED

- advertising fliers
- a report to present to advertisers
- an answering machine, preferably one that records onto a standard cassette or chip for better quality sound
- a dedicated phone line (used only for your business)

WHAT TO CHARGE

Callers do not pay for your information. Instead, advertisers pay you to run short commercials in conjunction with what people will hear on your line.

Charge advertisers $5.00 per day for a thirty-second advertisement. Try to run two advertisers a day.

START HERE

Here's how it works. Say you have a "Dial-a-Story" line. Someone calls and hears something like this: "Hello, thanks for calling the Dial-a-Story line. Today's story is brought to you by Twin Cities Toy Shop, which offers a complete selection of masks, face-paint, and costumes. Act out your favorite stories with all the trimmings from Twin Cities Toy Shop, located at 470 Searls Avenue. Call 123-4567 for more information. Now, for today's story . . ."

To make this business work, you have three main tasks. The first is to convince people to call your line so that the advertisers will have reason to advertise. The second is to sell the advertising time to small business owners in the community. The third is to gather and record new and interesting information every day.

Task #1: Convince people to call your line. Advertisers will only be interested in paying you for "airtime" if a lot of people are hearing their ads. Distribute fliers, make announcements at school and at church, run ads in the paper, hang posters around town. Be sure to let people know that the service itself is free. Get as many people calling as you can so you can tell advertisers that it's worth their money to advertise with you.

Task #2: Sell advertising time to business owners. Write a report that explains what you're doing. Put in samples of the information that people will hear on your info line. Write down how many people are calling your line and how many callers you expect to get in the next few months. Write down your strategy for getting the information out about your service. Put it all in a nice notebook and present this information to your potential advertisers. You will convince your advertisers that you're serious about success if you present yourself and your information in a neat, orderly way.

Task #3: Gather and record new information every day. The information you present, no matter what it is, must be of quality. Otherwise, people will call only once and give up. You want them to call daily, knowing that what they hear will be worth the time they spent calling. Be wise in your choices, remembering that everything you say reflects upon the advertiser. Be diligent about changing the message every morning; it will not take long. Enjoy developing this fun and fulfilling business!

TRICKS OF THE TRADE

Try to approach advertisers who have an interest in your information. If you present Bible verses or stories, ask members of your church who are business owners to advertise. They will be interested in spreading biblical truths to the community. If you run a joke line, ask bookstores, toy stores, novelty shops, and gift stores that sell humorous material to advertise with you. If your phone line is dedicated to featuring daily stories about student successes in your community, take your idea to the PTA; they may be interested in supporting your business. Certainly many parents who are business owners would want to contribute to such a morale-building idea. The kids at school would call every day to see who was featured on the line!

After you record your daily message, call it from another phone to make sure it is clear and understandable. Listen to the way radio announcers speak and learn to communicate slowly and enunciate clearly so your callers are never frustrated.

Take seriously your opportunity to provide enriching material to your community. Think of ways to use your info line to build others up. This business can be very creative and exciting, especially if it is used in both an honorable and enjoyable way.

PARENTAL GUIDANCE SUGGESTED

On paper, this endeavor sounds pretty complicated. In reality it is not. In fact, kids who are quite young could manage it with a little direction from you. If this is of interest to your child, help him first determine what kind of info line he wants to have. What does he want people to hear when they call? Having determined this to his (and your) satisfaction, the rest is fairly simple to plan. Brainstorm together on how to interest callers and how to approach potential advertisers. Support him as he draws up his proposal and begins meeting with business owners. It will help to set some long-term and short-term goals together. Help him see the advantages of planning toward preset objectives.

You may want to work out an arrangement regarding the phone line and answering machine. If he has no money to invest in those things and you choose to help him out, be sure you write a contract with specific provisions for repayment. Though parents often want to give their kids the world, in this instance, it will greatly benefit him to learn what a business arrangement is and how important it is to meet such obligations.

48

Clean Pools

Hard working, dependable kid needed to maintain pools and hot tubs.

WHAT YOU NEED

- advertising fliers
- a chemical testing kit, available from a pool supply store (optional)

WHAT TO CHARGE

$25.00 to $30.00 per month for weekly service.

FIND THE CUSTOMER

Circulate your fliers throughout the neighborhood. Ask the local pool supply store if you can leave fliers on the sales counter.

Go door to door, explaining your service. If someone tells you that they already use another company, ask them politely how much they pay for it. If you can undercut the price by at least $5.00, offer to do so, asking them to evaluate who does a better job after one month.

Talk with contractors who are building new homes and Realtors who are selling vacant homes. Offer to service the pool while the house is on the market. Chances are the new owner will keep you on.

START HERE

Make an appointment that you will keep on a weekly basis.

When you arrive for the first time, ask your customer to show you the equipment and the usual procedure. Listen closely so that you learn what your customer prefers. You'll be demonstrating respect as well.

There are four main components to pool cleaning.

1. *Skimming.* With a long-handled net, gently scoop up leaves, bugs, and other debris floating on the pool's surface.

2. *Sweeping.* Brush dirt off the sides and bottom into a central spot in the deep end of the pool.

3. *Vacuuming.* Hook up a long hose to the pool vacuum and vacuum the sides and bottom, sucking up the dirt pushed into the deep end by the sweeper.

4. *Testing.* Using a special kit, test the pool chemistry, adding necessary chemicals identified by the test.

The whole procedure takes about an hour. Hot tubs require basically the same procedure, except for the vacuuming.

TRICKS OF THE TRADE

Sometimes the hardest part of pool cleaning is dealing with the customer's dog. Ask permission to give the dog a treat every time you come. It may make your entry into the backyard a little easier.

When sweeping the dirt in the pool, push very slowly so the dirt remains settled on the bottom. If you push too fast, the dirt will dissipate into the water and settle back down to the bottom about an hour after you've left. Your customer will not be impressed.

Try to work a deal with the local pool supply store. Tell the owner that you will bring him all your business and will even pick up and deliver supplies if he will pay a commission on all he sells through you.

Always be prompt. If you will be late or unable to keep your appointment, it is crucial that you call your customer. Your integrity is at stake.

Offer additional services in your pool cleaning business. Learn to backwash the pool pump and change the diatomaceous earth in the filter system. This procedure should be done about four times a year for a charge of about $25.00. You can also scrub stains and algae from the pool surface with a special cleaning stone available at pool supply stores. Hot tubs need occasional water changes; tiles often need replacing; switches and buttons wear out. Be on the lookout for ways in which you can expand your service, making more money and helping your customer with your expertise.

PARENTAL GUIDANCE SUGGESTED

Often, kids who pursue this sort of job have had experience at home caring for a pool or a hot tub. If this is true in your case, take advantage of the opportunity to teach your child the inner workings of your pool system. The better he understands the big picture, the better he will be able to conduct his business. Any information you can collect and pass on to him will have a twofold benefit. He will gain knowledge, and he will see that you are committed to helping him succeed in his venture.

Although he must take responsibility for keeping his

appointments, you can help by buying him a large and colorful calendar that he can write on or an appointment book that he can carry with him. Notice out loud when he is faithfully prompt, and as he proves to be responsible, reward him with new privileges. Let him know that he is earning your trust by his actions. If he is not responsible, don't bail him out. Painfully, he will learn the hard way, and the lesson will most likely stick.

Help him think about what he can do to go the extra mile. Are there some other simple chores he can quietly do just to help his customer out? Can he bring a small seasonal gift or birthday card? Can he run an errand? Help him to see what satisfaction he can find in giving a little extra, especially when he sees the dramatic effect it has on his employer. This lesson learned now can change his life.

49

Wash Cars

Enthusiastic car washer needed to wash, wax, vacuum, and polish for grateful adults.

WHAT YOU NEED

- For washing—bucket, biodegradable liquid soap, a large number of rags
- For waxing—wax, more rags, a chamois

- For interior cleaning— dashboard cleaner, upholstery cleaner, or spot remover
- wagon or pushcart to transport your supplies

WHAT TO CHARGE

$8.00 per car for a basic wash and vacuum, $3.00 for waxing, $3.00 for detailing (cleaning dashboard, upholstery, tires, etc.).

FIND THE CUSTOMER

Take your supply wagon and go door to door. Hand the person a flier then introduce yourself. Tell her that you can take care of her car immediately. Tell her all you need is water and a vacuum cleaner.

When you're finished ask the customer if she would like you to come back again. If so, decide on a day. This way you can develop a base of regular customers.

Be sure to thank the person for giving you a chance, and when you speak, look the customer in the eye. People generally like and trust you more when you do.

START HERE

Washing a car is easy and fun. Pay attention to detail, and you'll do a great job. First squirt a small amount of soap into the bucket. Next, turn on the customer's hose, rinse down the car, and fill the bucket with water. Turn off the hose. (Don't ever let a customer's hose run freely while you're not using it. Most people pay for water, and hopefully, they're conservation-conscious as well.) Dip a rag in the sudsy water and scrub the car using a circular motion. Pay special attention to the nooks and crannies, especially in the front where bugs often meet their untimely demise. Rinse the soap off the car with the hose, making sure to send the suds down the driveway to the gutter. Dry the car using at least three rags. Now, you're through with the basic wash.

When working in the interior, be careful of the customer's possessions. Don't kneel on sunglasses or step on a pile of papers. Ask the customer to remove anything valuable before you begin.

When you've finished, put a flier on the dashboard or front seat with a chocolate candy on top. Your customer will be pleased with your good work and your thoughtfulness.

TRICKS OF THE TRADE

While you're washing, put a big free-standing sign on the sidewalk that reads "Car Cleaning Service by Drew Martin, age 12. Good Work. Good Prices. Call 123-7654."

If your customer owns a second car, offer to wash it for $6.00. It will be worth it since you don't have to transport your supplies or empty your soap bucket.

If your customer expresses appreciation or pleasure in your work, give her a few fliers and ask her to distribute them to people she knows. Let her know she can really help you and thank her for trying.

PARENTAL GUIDANCE SUGGESTED

Help ensure your child's success by training her thoroughly. Though car washing isn't on the same technological plane as brain surgery, there are pitfalls to avoid. Make sure, for instance, that your child knows to remove all the soap. Make sure she knows to close windows! Make sure she knows not to accidentally drench the customer when she forgets which way the hose is pointing.

Insist that she practice repeatedly. (At least your cars will be clean.) Even though she will be anxious to start "the real thing," don't be afraid to insist that she master her trade before going public.

Help her understand the value of taking pride in her work, of striving for excellence. Encourage her to take as much time as she needs to finish an outstanding job. If she learns to do her work with her whole heart, until it is done right, she will have learned something of inestimable value.

About the Authors

Todd Temple is the cofounder and executive director of 10 TO 20. He is the author or coauthor of ten books, including *52 Ways to Make This Your Best Year Yet*, *Answers to Everything*, and *How to Rearrange the World*.

Melinda Douros has a B.A. in English literature from Stanford University and is a graphic designer and scriptwriter.